AN OPEN DOOR:

New Travel Writing for
a Precarious Century

Steven Lovatt is the author of *Birdsong in a Time of Silence* (Particular Books, 2021), and over the last decade his critical articles on Welsh literature, particularly Dorothy Edwards, have been published in *New Welsh Review*, *Planet*, *Critical Survey*, the AWWE Yearbook and the *Literary Encyclopaedia*. He reviews poetry for *The Friday Poem*, teaches literature and creative writing at the University of Bristol, and copy-edits books on ethnography and philosophy from his home in Swansea.

AN OPEN DOOR:

New Travel Writing for
a Precarious Century

Edited by Steven Lovatt

PARTHIAN

Parthian, Cardigan SA43 1ED www.parthianbooks.com
First published in 2022
© the contributors 2022
ISBN 978-1-913640-62-0
Editor: Steven Lovatt
Cover design by Syncopated Pandemonium
Typeset by Elaine Sharples
Printed and bound by 4edge Limited, UK
Published with the financial support of the Welsh Books Council
British Library Cataloguing in Publication Data
A cataloguing record for this book is available from the British Library.

CONTENTS

INTRODUCTION

'Strange time to put together a travel book', said a friend, and there was no need to ask what she meant. In this early spring of 2022, the Covid-19 pandemic that emerged two years ago is still complicating travel to an extent barely fathomable to we Western post-war generations who had taken its possibility for granted. Amid the hardships and annoyances of separation from family members, postponed journeys and the reluctant acceptance of video 'meetings', the Covid-prompted necessity to rethink how and why we travel, and whether we should really do so as blithely as we once did, has coincided with other, interconnected and equally pressing emergencies.

Prior to the mid-twentieth century, leisured travel was largely the preserve of a wealthy elite, and it could easily become so again, even as the combined disasters of climate collapse, pandemic and persecution are displacing millions of people on journeys that they would never have wished for. The dream of global interconnectedness on free market terms exposes its contradictions at the moment of its greatest fulfilment.

The title of this anthology is borrowed from Jan Morris, who wrote to Owain Glyndŵr that 'if the mountains secluded Wales from England, the long coastline was like an open door to the world at large'. It was a strong and sudden sense of cultural loss and disorientation, prompted by the passing of Morris, which made me conceive the book as a sort of affirmation, and the image of an open door seems apt to contain all of the realities and possibilities that confront Wales in these dangerous times, from the door held open to refugees from Afghanistan to the Welsh government's proposals to dissuade its young people from seeking 'better prospects' beyond the country, and calls to defend Welsh identity from a new movement of monied incomers. All this in a context – not alien to Glyndŵr – of rising calls for self-determination and the recent sealing, unprecedented for centuries, of the Welsh–English border, albeit this time as a measure against the spread of Covid-19.

In light of all this, an anthology of travel and place writing seems, at second glance, perfectly timed. Indeed, from another angle it is long overdue, since to my knowledge, despite Wales having for centuries been written *about*, primarily as a sort of dream theatre for English aesthetes and capitalists, never before have Welsh and Wales-based authors been invited to 'write back' about their experiences as travellers within and beyond the country. *An Open Door* is also most likely one of the first travel anthologies in any language to have been published since the start of the pandemic and, notwithstanding the fully realised individuality of its stories, the distinctive anxieties of our age are everywhere apparent in what amounts in sum to a belated sea-change in the genre of travel writing itself.

This change is similar to those that have recently given new life to the closely related genre of nature writing. Historically, nature writing tended to overlook the historical and cultural specifics, the experiences and daily lives, of those who actually inhabit 'nature', while its exclusivity, related to a persistent privileging of the male 'expert', denied a voice to people – disproportionately women, children, the elderly and the otherwise culturally marginalised – who either hadn't the opportunity to roam and write at leisure or whose perspectives were simply not valued.

On a parallel track, it isn't all that difficult to see Wales as having been historically over-represented (and thus *mis*represented) by more or less voyeuristic and exoticising writers from elsewhere, nor to appreciate, as a consequence, the appropriateness of a Welsh challenge to what in travel writing, as in nature writing, is a Sunday-supplement-friendly hegemony of the soothing, 'uplifting' and unexceptional. *An Open Door* can certainly be interpreted as a challenge to this hegemony, and its contributors as representing, in the diversity of their backgrounds and experiences, a new and vitally necessary realism in the genre.

In 2022 we are quite obviously in all sorts of specific and unprecedented trouble, and this is directly acknowledged by almost all of this book's stories. In Sophie Buchaillard's 'Revolving Doors', the face coverings that she and her son are obliged to wear on public transport find an apocalyptic echo in famous Parisian landmarks screened behind scaffolding and other concealments: 'Everywhere, tourists marvel at the audio description of buildings hidden behind plastic sheets. It is as if we are too late'. The sense of civilisation at bay is also present in references to social violence and terrorism in Brazil and Somalia, while in Mary-Ann Constantine's 'King Stevan's

Roads', a story about how history adds layers to our sense of place also ends (or rather breaks off) in a Paris under siege.

Everywhere in the anthology, personal stories are given weight and depth by an awareness of history and politics, from the grim carceral tradition of British asylums to the enriching cultural hybridity made possible, for example, by the National Coal Board's post-war recruitment drive in Italy, as revealed by Giancarlo Gemin's moving memoir of his mother. Faisal Ali's 'From the Desert to the Docks and Back' traces a narrative across four generations of the author's family, providing glimpses along the way of almost two centuries of personal, national and global history, while in 'Clearances', Kandace Siobhan Walker witnesses at first hand both the effects of forced displacement and the tenacious love that exists between people and their ancestral homelands.

The collection extends individual experience in other ways, too. It is striking how many of these stories feature children and, more broadly, intergenerational relationships, and it is made clear how love of one's places, whether native or adopted, implies guardianship and what Alan Garner has called 'the subtle matter of owning and being owned' by one's landscapes, cities, religions and cultures. In 'Gone to Abergavenny', Grace Quantock finds solace in a place to which, as she is all too well aware, she would once have been forcibly confined, and for Siân Melangell Dafydd, the lived history of her family in a particular sacred landscape affords sanctuary for both herself and the next generation.

But for all the awareness, displayed throughout this anthology, of the weight of history we carry within ourselves, and which can't help but inflect our perceptions, our assessments and our stories, *An Open Door* is no less a showcase of its contributors' individual personalities in all their insightfulness and irony, eccentricities and humour. We learn a lot about the experience of travel itself. Several of the stories touch on the sheer awkwardness of being a stranger in a strange land, but also how this needn't at all contradict a deep appreciation, both of the unfamiliar place itself and of how exposure to it can disarm us in ways both frightening and delightful. As Eluned Gramich expresses it in 'Carioca Cymreig', 'It's one of the pleasures of travel to submit yourself to other people, to let yourself be guided and taught', while in 'The Murmuration', Julie Brominicks' acknowledgement of her loneliness as a foreigner gives way movingly and with great psychological truth to sudden and unexpected confessions of 'love [for] this place, and these people'.

A less apparent, though equally present, insight of this book is that the relationship between people and places is two-way: that is to say, in order to thrive, places also need their people. In 'From Light and Language and Tides', Neil Gower charts, literally as well as figuratively, a journey that begins with a professional interest in a poet's attachment to his landscape and ends with a series of personal revelations about the different ways in which fidelities of all kinds are grounded in a relationship with inherited and discovered places. Similar questions about how journeys are bound up with loyalty and duty are explored in E. E. Rhodes' 'All Among the Saints', which is also one of several pieces that demonstrate with wit, honesty and compassion how travel to even relatively nearby destinations can nevertheless involve the work of a lifetime.

Taken together, the stories of *An Open Door* extend Jan Morris' legacy into a turbulent present and an even more uncertain future. In doing so, and by the sheer intellectual entertainment they provide, they not only irrigate Welsh literary culture, but affirm all cultures and individuals that still value the curiosity and humility proper to travel, and the deepening of one's relationships with places and their inhabitants. Whether seen from Llŷn or the Somali desert, we still take turns to look out at the same stars, and it might be this recognition, above all, that encourages us to hold the door open for at least a while longer yet.

Steven Lovatt, 6 January 2022

ELUNED GRAMICH

Carioca Cymreig

Santa Teresa, Rio de Janeiro
New Year's Eve 2018

It was the first time we saw the New Year in together. We stood on a balcony overlooking the city and the favela Santa Marta below: a wild garden ran down into small white buildings, bare bricks, a thousand electric lights. Rio's outline bloomed with fireworks, and we watched the sparkling nets raining on the city. I remembered how in Welsh we say *tân gwyllt*, 'wild fire', for these marvels, and in Japan they say *hanabi*, 'fire flowers', and I was reminded of how beautiful fireworks can be, but also of their power to lift us out of the grooves of our ordinary experiences.

'Can you hear that?' R said to me. He was smiling in the excitable way that means he is about to teach me something. 'That *tak-tak-tak* sound?'

'You mean the fireworks.'

He shook his head. 'No! It's guns from the favela. The drug cartels are shooting into the air to celebrate.'

I backed away, immediately thinking of those stories I'd been told. The one about the cleaner at R's university who was shot by a stray bullet while working on the campus. Or the story of the woman sitting up in bed with her partner, looking at her phone, when she was shot in the head by accident.

'Don't worry,' he said. 'It's safe here.'

I turned to see R's friends sitting around a platter of white chocolate *brigadeiros*, drinking cold beer out of small glasses. The stories faded from my mind. This often happened to me in Rio: I had the luxury of forgetting, of turning away from violence and politics to watch fireworks from a balcony, taste the coconut and *doce de leite*, accept the sparkler that was handed to me and with which I spelled our names in the air.

I also had the luxury of ignorance. It's one of the pleasures of travel to submit yourself to other people, to let yourself be guided and taught. Usually, you're expected to play the adult in life, but as a visitor with only a basic grasp of Portuguese, nothing was expected of me except perhaps politeness and patience. I didn't even know how to celebrate New Year's Eve properly. I'd brought a black dress decorated with colourful flowers with me from west Wales. Wearing black, I was quickly told, is unlucky. My mother-in-law – a woman half my size – cajoled me into wearing her clothes for the night: a long white skirt and a gold, glittering top that barely fitted. Earlier that day she'd forced a tiny camisole over my head. I got completely stuck, the nylon gluing to my hot, sweaty skin, and it was only with great effort that she managed to prise it over my shoulders. Camisole or not, I adhered to tradition. The colour you wear on New Year's Eve represents your hopes for the coming year: yellow or gold for money, white for peace, red for passion, green for health and orange for happiness. (A year later, when R and I marry in Cardiff, I will forget to tell the Brazilians that black is unlucky for weddings in Wales. Our wedding photos show one side of the family in bright summer frocks, and the other side in black suits and cocktail dresses).

I sat down with R's friends, joining the row of white and gold, and tried to follow their quick Portuguese while the machine guns from Santa Marta fired into the night sky.

***

Barra, Rio de Janeiro
18–21 December 2018

Deixe-me ir	Let me go
preciso andar	I must wander
Vou por aí a procurar	I'll go around searching
rir pra não chorar	Laugh so I won't cry
Deixe-me ir	Let me go
preciso andar	I must wander
Vou por aí a procurar	I'll go around searching
rir pra não chorar	Laugh so I won't cry

Cartola – 'Preciso me encontrar'

I suppose this is a practical kind of love story. The story of how things were going to work for R and I, between Aberystwyth and Rio de Janeiro. When you marry outside your nationality, you are bound not only to the person but also to their culture. It becomes part of your life. My Welsh mother married my German father and, I think, she didn't know then that this would mean spending the rest of her life travelling to and from Munich, celebrating Christmas on Christmas Eve, learning and unlearning German on an annual cycle, hearing my father's never-ending complaints about British bread. And so, when I fell in love with R, I absorbed the stories of his life and also the stories of his country, the Carioca stories – Carioca being the term for someone from Rio de Janeiro.

In our first weeks together, I had Chico Buarque, Cartola, Nelson Goncalves playing repeatedly on my phone: those old samba men of Brazilian song, crooning into my ears as I walked the Aberystwyth promenade. I didn't understand a word of their lyrics. I assumed anything they sang was heart-rendingly romantic (and not, as it later transpired, intensely political). I paused my own studies to read a multi-volume history of Brazil while sitting on a bench at Aber marina, looking across at the blue-and-green fishing vessels coming in from Cardigan Bay, dreaming of how I would soon be exchanging Tan-y-Bwlch for Copacabana. I read Machado de Assis while staying with my parents that final Christmas without R: the surreal *The Posthumous Memoirs of Bras Cubas*, which made no sense to me at all at the time, as a political satire of nineteenth-century Brazilian society, and was hardly romantic, but which nevertheless made me feel closer to him.

It finally happened in December 2018: my first visit to Brazil to meet R's family provided a warm, blue-skied view of my future. Here were the people I would meet year in and year out; here was the language I would listen to every day, either in person or on a WhatsApp call; here was the food that would be kept in the kitchen for the rest of my life, and the Brazilian shops I would be searching out (Where can you buy *feijão preto* in Wales? And what about fresh cassava root? Is there no dendé oil in this country?) We were on the plane and then we were in São Paulo, in a very long queue for our connecting flight, holding two over-priced cartons of *pao de queijo*. And I was terribly sick.

'You gave me this,' I said. R had been ill just before the flight. I ran around the enormous, chaotic airport, looking for a pharmacy. Where was Boots? 'I can't believe you gave me your cold. I hate you.'

'I can't believe you spent seventy reias on *pão de queijo*,' he replied. 'Do you know how much seventy reias is in pounds?'

I stuck another greasy ball of cheese bread into my mouth. 'I could do with about a hundred more of them.'

We arrived late in Rio. R's father picked us up and I sat in the back, eyes half-closed, pain tightening around my head, hoping no one would speak to me. I had met his parents once before when they visited Aberystwyth during Easter; but that had been different, taking them around a place I knew well. Here, I would be the one to submit, listen, follow in half-understanding.

My father-in-law is the same height as R, silver-haired, stocky, immaculately dressed. For him, everything must always be clean. The car is spotless. He has two showers a day, at least. R takes after his mother's Lebanese side, having a mop of black curls and dark brown eyes, while his father is fairer, more Italianate. He doesn't speak very much English, but he will speak to me anyway. He will say my name followed by one English word – 'you', say, or 'today' – and then he will um and ah because he has forgotten what words should follow the first word. Then he slips back into Portuguese, smiling, and pretending that I understand, and I pretend I understand too. Sometimes I do, but whether we understand each other or not is quite unimportant. This is something that people learning a foreign language may not realise: it doesn't matter if you

11

understand, or if you make yourself understood. It's the effort to speak and understand that counts the most. Showing the other person that you would like to communicate with them, even if means utterly embarrassing yourself in the process, is the highest expression of kindness and affection. And so every time my father-in-law says, 'Eluned, you, today, um, ah...,' I like him more.

'Eluned, you okay? *Tudo bem?*'

'*Tudo. Obrigada.*' 'Fine, thank you', although I felt like I was dying. I closed my eyes, listened to the calming hum of the air conditioner. I so wanted to make a good impression! To look nice for the family. R's relatives are all so beautiful. Some of them are actual models! My nose throbbed, bright red.

The sun was sinking slowly. On either side of the road was a sprawl of low houses and, beyond the houses, the Atlantic Ocean, melting into the horizon. The yellow-pink of the sunset reflected in the water.

And then Barra – the Miami of Rio de Janeiro. We passed Barra Shopping (the biggest shopping centre in Latin America!), lines of palm trees, huge roads with no pavements. The architecture of the middle-classes in Rio is tall white apartment blocks, crowded together into neighbourhoods that share a local supermarket, parks, a swimming pool and, most importantly, security. These are gated areas where it is forbidden to hang your washing out to dry because it would look too much like a favela, or so I was told. Many apartments are unoccupied for most of the day, populated only by maids who clean and cook and change the sheets. Layers of security slowed our journey: guards in square outhouses, like a border check, glanced at R's father's identity card. Later, I had to go to the offices in R's apartment complex to obtain a special visitor card, so that I would be able to wander the complex freely and use the swimming pool outside their building that R and his parents had never used themselves.

The apartment was white and incredibly clean: sharp lines, glass furniture, the tiled floors gleaming; living room, two bedrooms, balcony, kitchen and, behind the kitchen, a small room where the *empregada*, or housemaid, lived from Monday to Friday. R's room had been cleared of most of his teenage accoutrements – only a few items remained to reflect his eccentric interest in English history, including a framed copy of the Magna Carta on the wall and a newspaper print headlining the start of the Second World War. The room was small and cool; there was a single bed with white sheets on which I immediately curled up, hoping the paracetamol would kick in. Even in my head-cold state, the perfect cleanliness of the apartment awed me – *ironed sheets!* – and made me think of the inexorable labour that underpinned it. A woman had done this for me and R: a woman I didn't know had cleaned, ironed, folded and ordered all of R's clothes. She had swept the dust from his empty desk, the tops of his books.

'What's her name again? Your maid?'

'Irene. She's not a maid,' R said, pulling a clean shirt over his head. 'Well, I suppose, she is and she isn't. I call her my second mother. She looked after me while my parents worked. I used to "help" her clean the apartment when I was a toddler. You'll meet her on Monday.'

'Where does she live when she's not here?'

'Realengo. It's an area outside the city. It's normal for the help to live out in the suburbs and travel in for the week. Or they commute for hours every day on buses. They get up at five and arrive home at eleven.' He stuck his wallet in his back pocket. 'Remember, you can talk about anything but politics with my family. Don't mention Bolsonaro.'

I rolled onto my back, stared up at the ceiling. 'Can I stay here?'

'Are you sure? I mean, that's fine, but my aunt and uncle are expecting you.'

My head and face ached; a tissue was scrunched up in both hands. 'No. I'll come.'

***

R's aunt lived in a gated complex too. We took the lift up to the flat where the whole family were eating and drinking (not the *whole* family, I was later informed, but a small sub-section of it): R's brother, sister-in-law, two cousins and their partners, and five-year-old twin girls with their hair in bunches. Everybody embraced and kissed me, even though I was obviously sick and spent most of the evening going back and forth to the toilet for more tissues. His aunt ushered me into the kitchen to show me her handmade gnocchi and I did my best not to sneeze on anything. The food was served on enormous silver platters, and R's sister-in-law, an acclaimed chef, ate the food slowly and deliberately, as though we were sampling a tasting menu in a high-end restaurant. R piled the food high on his plate and asked me what I thought of it – wasn't his aunt the best cook in the world? He was excited – smiling and laughing at everything, accepting one whisky after another from his equally cheerful uncle. It had been a year since he'd seen them; it made me happy to see him so animated and confident after a year of negotiating the world in his second language.

Meeting your partner's family when you don't share a common language is a gift, especially if you're an introvert. You don't need to make conversation; your role is to smile and eat and compliment the food. You can pass a pleasant half an hour together simply by asking what the words are for the food you have been given and repeating them wrongly. Language is replaced with touch – especially in Brazil, where hugs and kisses for greeting are the norm. I ate the gnocchi and the dessert of *goiabada*, a paste of guava and sugar, and said it was delicious, and smiled as best I could, and waited patiently for the conversations (and the whiskies) to come to an end.

R's brother and sister-in-law drove us back. On going up another steep road, his brother turned and said to me: 'Just look at these hilly streets! I bet you don't have hills like this in Wales.'

***

There's a certain zeal that comes with showing someone around your country, your city. The longer I played the tourist, the more my foreignness expanded and intensified. For R's family I quickly transformed into a person who didn't know very much about anything, because I hadn't experienced the world through Brazil. I didn't know about hills, for instance. Or fish ('This is *bacalhau* – cod. Have you had cod before?'). Or beaches. Or healthcare. If I'd been younger, I would have found this infuriating, but I've learned that the impulse behind such enthusiastic tour-guiding is kind. These comments came from the sincere desire to include me in the culture, and the understandable desire to hear praise and love for that culture, too: love I was only too happy to give as we walked through the city, me taking notes on my phone as I went. I loved, for example, the wall at Urca, waist-high and built of stone, that skims the Baia de Guanabara, where people gather at dusk to watch the sunset, drink cold beer and watch the fishing boats sail in and out. I loved the Rio mountains that emerge impossibly from the centre of the city, like green thumbs erupting through the dull colours of the residential districts. And I loved Cristo Redentor's silvery form against the sky.

We took the train to visit him. It was so hot, and the flight of steps that led to the foot of the statue so long, that I thought I would collapse. We stopped at the fruit juice stall so that I could drink *mamão*, sweet pink-orange pulp in a glass, and then I tried, one by one, the rest of the juices I could not drink at home: *caju* and *cupuaçu* and avocado with milk, which was what R drank as a child like I drank banana-flavoured Nesquik. Later, I loved it when R's friend draped a garland of plastic pouches around my body and ordered 'Drink!', which I did. I loved, also, the bowls of cold açai which we ate with long spoons. And in between the trains to the tops of the green thumbs, the too-blue ocean, the beaches and the beach-seller who said '*Muchas Gracias!*' to me because I was foreign and they were the only foreign words I knew. I loved the coconut water and the meanders through the vast shopping centres where we bought our wedding rings. I heard all the stories of kidnap and theft and guns and they seemed nothing more than bad dreams.

'It can't happen here,' I said.

And R replied, 'You're blind.'

***

R's mother – a great believer in making life easier through purchase power – bought a tea Nespresso machine for my stay. Every morning I placed a capsule of green tea into the machine and watched it turn a simple ritual into something extremely complex. R made fun of his mother – 'You know that's the most expensive and ridiculous way of making tea, right?' – but I quietly enjoyed the weirdness of preparing it this way. In the mornings, R's mother would leave for work at the radiology clinic before seven, leaving R and I in the kitchen to have our breakfast with Irene, the *empregada*. His semi-retired father would come in, to say hello, hear our plans for the day or simply continue my education. 'Did you know,' he told me more than once, 'that Portuguese is much harder than Spanish? We understand eighty per cent of what they say but they don't understand eighty per cent of what we say!'

All the while, Irene made egg and tapioca for R. I couldn't ask for one because I knew it entailed work, and so I preferred to eat pieces of yesterday's ice-cream cake, or drink the glass of papaya and banana juice R's father blended for me when he heard about that hot day on Cristo Redentor where the *mamão* had saved me from fainting. Irene was at the stove, waiting for the tapioca flour to cook before folding it over. She is a small woman, over seventy years old, with dyed-black hair and thick-rimmed glasses. Whenever I was alone in the apartment with her, Irene talked to me as though I were Brazilian: she didn't bother to slow her speech or throw in English words. She had faith that we could understand each other. She mostly asked about food – what Brazilian food I liked, what I ate in Wales;

once, when I cooked an apple crumble for the family, she stood at my side in the kitchen, hands on hips, watching my every move. From R, she wanted to know about social media, emails, the whole technological world that she couldn't quite follow. That morning, after preparing R's egg and tapioca, Irene showed him her phone and asked him how she could use it to communicate with the new priest at her church. R talked her through it, reading aloud this or that instruction, and the messages and notifications she'd received.

Since my visit, Irene often sends me images of candles or flower-strewn cherubs with the message *Deus te abençoê* – God bless you.

***

Muriaé, Minas Gerais
21–23 December 2018

Earlier that year, the Virgin Mary had visited Dona Maria, R's ninety-year-old grandmother, for three days. The whole town had come to watch her through the windows, as she glided through the rooms of Dona Maria's house, through the spacious dining room where the neighbours gather to gossip, the kitchen where one of Dona Maria's seven children was cooking beef and polenta mash, past the photographic displays of infant grandchildren, to the veranda where Dona Maria spends her days watching the street. The Virgin Mary looked very happy in her temporary home: she gazed benignly at a corner of the best room of the house, 'the visitor's room', where she was visible to the whole street, her slender hands held up in prayer, until it was time for her to leave and return to the church until next year.

Dona Maria showed me the pictures of the annual parade of the Virgin Mary when we arrived at her house in Muriaé after driving four hours inland from Rio de Janeiro. Her house stood along one of the main streets, although there wasn't much in the way of traffic, the town being quiet and slow. Away from the breezes of the coast, the air in rural Minas Gerais lay heavily across my skin, like sodden clothes; when I met Dona Maria, I was flushed red and covered in a sheen of sweat. Still, she kissed me, then held my hands as I said *Bença* – 'Give me your blessing' – as I'd been instructed to do as a sign of respect. She proceeded to bless me in a rush of lyrical-sounding Portuguese in which I only understood the words bless, God, and *minha filha* – my daughter.

It was in Muriaé, more than anywhere else I'd been, that my poor Portuguese made no difference to how I was treated. I sat at the long dining table for hours, with neighbours on either side of me – old women, mostly, or distant cousins, or friends of cousins – who spoke to me at length about their lives, punctuated by concerned enquiries about my comfort, since there was no air-conditioning in the house apart from the bedrooms. I survived the heat, although not without ducking into the bedroom at hourly intervals. Each time I emerged, Dona Maria would be there to show me something new: a picture of her husband, a coffin-maker and town councillor, a man who was loved by everyone and who regularly visits R in his dreams; her nine children, all born in the house, two of whom died at birth because they were twins; a religious painting from one of her grandchildren; a picture of one of her grown-up granddaughters, a vet who was shot dead by an armed robber in a Muriaé clothes shop; the table full of wedding pictures of R's older cousins which R and I would soon join.

***

Apesar de você	In spite of you
Amanhã há de ser	Tomorrow will be
Outro dia	Another day
Eu pergunto a você	I ask you
Onde vai se seconder	Where you will hide
Da enorme euforia	From our happiness
Como vai proibir	How will you forbid
Quando o galo insistir	the cockerel
Em cantar	From singing
Água nova brotando	Spring water flowing
E a gente se amando	And the people loving each other
Sem parar	With no end in sight.

Chico Buarque – 'Apesar de Vocé'

Barra, Rio de Janeiro
New Year's Day 2019

We gathered in the Barra apartment to watch Jair Bolsonaro's inauguration; everyone in the room had voted for him apart from R. Months earlier, we had gone together to the embassy in London so that he could cast his vote, since voting is compulsory in Brazil. In the queue, R had made friends with another couple while I'd eaten several *coxinhas* from the pop-up Brazilian food stands off Trafalgar Square.

20

'Did you vote for him in the end?' R's brother asked him.

'No, I spoiled my ballot. They were both bad,' R lied. He'd voted for the other candidate, Haddad, the 'communist'.

We sat in a semi-circle around the television, watching Bolsonaro drive around in a black soft-top with his blonde wife as though they were both on their way to the altar.

'Who did Irene vote for?' I asked R quietly.

'Bolsonaro.'

'Why? He won't do anything for her.'

'No, but my parents will vote for him, and that's good enough. He's the only person she hears about on a regular basis.'

The triumphant music blasted through the living room. Bolsonaro received a sash in the colours of the Brazilian flag and became the President, while I desperately wished someone would pour me another glass of wine. R's mother and aunt cheered and clapped, while R looked strained, uncertain.

'Well, that's that,' he said.

It was strange to share in a celebration that I did not believe in. We both waited avidly for the guests to leave, for the little party to be over. It was strange, too, to feel the strangled emotions in the air – the collision between giddy hopefulness and anxious despair. We didn't know then what would happen in the next two years: how the thin, chinless man waving on the screen would be accused of committing genocide against his own people by denying the pandemic, or how he would spend his time in office gearing up for a military coup. It was good that we did not know all this as we finally cleared away the plates and said goodbye at the door.

'See you at the wedding!' they said, as they left.

'Are your parents happy we're getting married?' I asked R that

21

evening, one of the last days we would spend in his small, white room. 'Your brother and aunt and parents?'

'Very.'

'And you?'

'Excuse me?'

'I just want to double-check. You're happy to swap Copacabana for Cardigan Bay?'

R looked as though he was considering it. 'Yes. There's Bolsonaro. And I hate beaches, especially the sand. It gives me anxiety.'

'Are you even Brazilian?'

'Good question,' he said. 'Anyway, dwi'n dysgu Cymraeg. I'm ready for Wales.'

'A Welsh Carioca... Carioca Cymreig,' I said. 'I guess that's what you'll be.'

GRACE QUANTOCK

Gone to Abergavenny

In Abergavenny, in the old asylum grounds, I sit in my sea-green wheelchair under a copse of chestnut trees so tall they probably stood on this slope when the asylum was in its heyday in the 1850s. Old-growth trees surround what's left of the asylum walls, or where the walls used to stand. It smells green here; the lawns are mossy underfoot, the rough grass still wet. The ground under my wheels is a mix of coarse grass and clover. Dandelions lengthen at the edges where lawns meet a network of footpaths encircling the building. I can see dark specks of violets in the shade of a monkey puzzle tree which stands taller than the asylum building itself. I can feel the effect of being in this place, of being in a timeless bubble; it seems almost soporific, or perhaps it is just the absence of agitation that I usually feel when I am alone in the outside world.

The asylum opened at the end of 1851, built of red sandstone in a Gothic style. Its frontage has now faded to a muted coral, with creamy gold Bath stone framing the windows and lining the corners. It stretches across 500 feet and held 1,770 patients at its full capacity. It closed in 1997, by which time it was known as Pen-Y-Fal Hospital. Set on wide lawns, the building is ringed with these trees which today loom over even the asylum's imposing height.

Sitting close to the crumbled remains of the walls, within what would have been the asylum's grounds, I can hear the bubbling coos of wood pigeons, a descant of a blackbird in the copse behind me and a broader chorus of birdsongs I can't pick out. The interwoven chirps and warbles let me know there are no other humans nearby. The chorus has been building all the while I've been sitting here, and now it comes from all sides, ebbing and rising, like binaural beats. A column of sound encircles me. To be surrounded by birdsong after a year and a half indoors, after a decade housebound, with a year of that time in my bed, feels like an immersion in sound. I can hear a mower in the distance, the river Gavenny rippling over rocks in the riverbed down a sharp bank to the west. I can't hear any cars. It smells green here, fresh. A breeze is blowing cool off the river behind me, lapping my back through the silk of my blouse.

The rough lawns here are hard for my wheelchair, but it's flat enough that I can still bump over. The paths are stone rolled to dust, my favourite surface because it's accessible but still has the texture of dirt when I roll over it. As a wheelchair user, I'm very attuned to the textures of the ground. I have to think about it all the time. I'm closer to it, I rely on it and if I miscalculate, I can end up on it. I'm connected to path materials in a way many ambulatory visitors may not be, unless they too have to calculate their movements and how to get safely from one space to another.

Often, we think of access and adaptation as being smooth – tarmac, paving stones – yet while it's thrilling to soar over polished expanses like marble in a silky glide that reminds me of running, it still doesn't feel like being outside. Outside to me is earth, soil, mud – the huff of leaf mould under a boot, cushioned pine needles and the tang of sap in forestry plantations, a perceptible give of sand with every stride along the bay. I have to balance the sensory experiences of these spaces with what makes it possible for me to access them in the first place. I grew up traversing paths of ground stone along the Monmouthshire and Brecon canal, and I still love its reliable evenness and its slight grit beneath the tyres that reminds me I am outside.

Part of the attraction of green space is that it has the potential to ground us. To feel our feet on the earth is supposed to be calming and regulating. It can link us to the here and now, especially if we are getting lost in a storm of past pain and possible suffering inside our minds. Feet on the ground is today. It's the trouble of now, as bad as it is, not a lifetime of pain. But I can't put my feet on the ground; they sit on my wheelchair's footplate. Even if I transfer to a bench and manage to sit upright, putting my feet on the ground has a limited effect because I can't feel them fully. Instead, I think about what I *can* feel. My wheelchair is, to me, an extension of my body (that's why I don't like strangers touching it). It's made of aluminium hydroformed castor-link tubes. The aluminium is mined from the earth, so my wheelchair is made of what the earth is made of. My wheels have rubber tyres, derived from the sap of the rubber tree. I may not be putting my feet on the ground, but I sit within a part of the earth – the trees, the natural world – every day. My hands move over the same elements that make up our earth every time I move, even if my feet can't pace the ground.

I follow the soft path downwards. The asylum sits in a natural hollow; the paths circling it end in steps, wide and shallow, up and down the surrounding slopes. The steps have most likely been built for the retiree community who live in the converted asylum. They're easy enough to shuffle my wheelchair up and down, but there are ramps too. Ramps always instigate such a feeling of welcome in me: 'Ah, there are my people here. They've thought about me.' I can avoid the demeaning process of being dragged backwards up a high doorstep, or bracing for the scary process of jumping myself up a curb. I can do it: tip my wheelchair back, hook my front wheels onto the higher level and drag myself up by my left arm, pushing hard on my wheel. But if I miscalculate, I'll tip backwards. That's why hospitals fit all wheelchairs with anti-tippers, black bars with tiny wheels which protrude from the backs of the chairs. They rattle with every move. Many wheelchair users rip our anti-tippers off as soon as we get out of hospital. Because anti-tippers are so low to the ground, it's impossible to get up anything other than a fully dropped curb. Where these aren't to be found, I choose between the risk of falling or of getting stuck in the road. I'd rather try and fall safely than dodge traffic. But with ramps, these concerns diminish.

This is a gentle place. The only person I've spoken to today was a well-presented elderly white person in a cream Panama hat and an ivory linen suit, heading down into town for a daily constitutional. They offered a polite 'Good morning' on the way, and left me to my own devices. Earlier, I saw an older couple being shown around by a younger person in black. They stopped walking when they saw me, their eyes repeatedly raking me head to toe. I'm not sure if it's my wheelchair or my outfit. I love vintage, and today I'm wearing a houndstooth tweed shooting skirt from the 1940s and an apricot silk blouse from the late 1930s. Maybe the Victorian silk parasol was a bit much, but I didn't consider the impact my outfit would have set against a Victorian building. I am never out in the summer without a parasol because I burn so easily. When others are wearing as little as possible, I am adding layers of linen and SPF50 which I import from Japan. I'm never without a sun hat and parasol. I wear dresses and skirts exclusively. As a wheelchair user, sitting in jeans can mean skin damage from the pocket rivets and the thick, inflexible seams and, besides, sitting in a wheelchair for six hours in skinny jeans is horribly uncomfortable.

The asylum building before me is made of red stones, each slightly curved. The stones are irregularly shaped but fit together with the pleasingly balanced asymmetry of a drystone wall. It feels like I could sleep here, in this sling of birdsong, the occasional clatter of wings taking flight above me. There's a pleasant sense of being far from anyone, and from anything I might be required to do. Asylums were built with high walls to preclude escape; here they exist only in remnants, cut down to a comfortable height. But for me, at least, there's still a sense of moving beyond and between worlds when I enter the grounds. Maybe some of it is the cost: a flat in this converted asylum sells for £143,000, a townhouse in the newly converted asylum chapel for £485,000. These grounds aren't going to feel like the council estate in the valleys I live on (and love). There's spaciousness here, a graciousness of dimension. There will be grief and loneliness present, of course. The mundanity of Wi-Fi connections and overdue bills – the everyday struggles which strew our lives exist in these apartments too, but somehow seem diluted by these spacious old stones. The building is arranged with so much attention, and in complementary colouring of pink, cream and gold.

My partner, L, first introduced me to the asylum. He was having psychotherapy for mental health difficulties in Abergavenny and wandered along the river after a session one day, trying to clear his head. He followed the riverbank up a steep slope and walked into the wide, solitary asylum grounds. He brought me there the next day, but I found the location disquieting. Why would my beloved want to take me to a place where people like me had been locked up? People like him too. What could possibly be here for us? The answer, I found then, was solace.

I came to love the asylum grounds for their sanctuary, and for the tranquility I found there. On return visits I took my laptop and wrote in the shelters that dot the grounds – an odd working space, but one that suited me for its quiet. I took L there when he was ill, when his meds weren't working and we'd exhausted our options. Wide, quiet outdoor spaces seemed to be the only thing that would bring him back to himself. When I was exhausted from long nights without sleep while he was in an episode, I would become desperate to escape the tight walls of our flat and the aloneness we experienced when surrounded by people as powerless as ourselves. I learned later that for many years the phrase 'gone to Abergavenny' was used as a euphemism for being committed to the asylum. After its closure, the Grade II listed asylum building fell into disrepair and was later converted for housing and renamed Sarno Square. Many of the asylum properties were demolished and the grounds built over. The asylum was of the type whose wards all branched off one long corridor. Men's and women's wards were strictly segregated. It initially held 210 'inmates' in seventy-two wards, and was set in seventy-five acres of landscaped grounds.

I've wondered why we go to the grounds of an old asylum at all – to what is today a private housing estate. It seems a strange place for me to seek solace, committed as I am to freedom. I think I go for the same reason I haunted churchyards and burial grounds during the Covid-19 lockdowns: for space and solitary time. It's hard to find quiet when my body is seen as a curiosity. In my local park, I get asked questions about my wheelchair, and my partner, who is often the only Brown person we see, is asked where he is from: 'No, where are you really from? But where are your parents from?' My therapist said maybe L is looking for asylum, a place to be when he is too sick to handle the world. We are not alone in this struggle: seven million people in Wales and England – one in six adults – are said to have significant psychiatric problems. One third of families have a member who is mentally ill at some point.

I'm not the only one to appreciate the sense of space, relief and respite which still permeates these grounds. The new residents, too, have expressed how peaceful it is, despite initial misgivings over the former use of the building. I'm grateful for my aloneness here. No one asks me what's wrong with me. My existence isn't policed or politicised. The difficulties disabled people face in accessing green space aren't so much about a lack of ramps as the rebuking we get when we arrive there. And our options are usually so few. There are two parks near my council estate – we are lucky – but the one on the estate itself is little more than a fenced-off football pitch that's been behind Harris panels for two years now. It has a tiny playpark of swings and slides on rotting tarmac scattered with broken glass. There's a potholed path between the playground and the pitch. No benches, no view, nowhere for me to go. The second park, outside the estate, has neat-edged ornamental flower beds, a bowling green and a tennis court, and is crammed with people. I appreciate the community aspect, but during lockdown I craved space. Not to wriggle through crowds for my tiny piece of shade with scores of strangers. We were all seeking something on the pocket-handkerchief-sized green space allotted us. In summer the parks get crowded and queues form on the canal towpaths. I realise how much of the countryside has been built over.

Even at the asylum, only a fragment of the original 75 acres of landscaped grounds remains, most of it having been built over. But there are still quiet streets of pink townhouses with well-tended gardens, hydrangeas, white roses, wisteria and, of course, a view of an eighteenth-century 'lunatic asylum'. It's an oddly restful vista. And what's left of the grounds is enclosed by trees with views of mountains all around. The modern housing estates beyond the asylum grounds feel at more than a physical distance. The sentinel trees are a mix of monkey puzzles, laurels and pines. Some are so old I initially mistake them for redwoods; their trunks are so thick, with deep-scored bark folds. The grove of chestnuts stands behind the main asylum building. I could have been sent here then, but I am here now by choice, seeking out a landscape I can access – that I fit in and that fits me.

I am of the first generations of disabled people in Wales not routinely institutionalised. If I had entered the asylum when it was an active psychiatric institution, I would first have passed through the large gates by the porter and his lodge, which still stands at Abergavenny. If allowed to, I may have paused to glance behind me as I passed inside the walls; I would have had a sense of going beyond, leaving the everyday world behind, entering another country. The asylum building would have been dominated by a water tower at the centre of the grounds. As I passed through the gates, I would have seen the asylum chapel to my left, with its gleaming copper bell tower. Grouped around the water tower would have been kitchens, laundries, workshops, an administrative block and a recreation hall; these were often designed like churches or ballrooms.

The recreation hall at Abergavenny held a grand piano, and staff remember nightly concerts given by talented patients; a baritone singer whose name has not survived was reported as a favourite entertainer. Asylums were worlds unto themselves, surrounded by high walls and in rural settings, without the encroachment of houses that now lap at their borders. The asylum gardens were often designed by highly capable landscape gardeners. They were intended simultaneously as places of tranquility and confinement. The grounds held orchards, farms to provide food for the asylum, workshops, bowling greens, cricket pitches and croquet lawns. Many had 'airing courts' next to the wards, where patients could exercise in walled gardens. It's easy to imagine how welcome the relative freedom of the gardens would have been, in contrast to the wards where up to fifty patients slept in each dormitory. Asylums were effectively independent communities, with their own hairdressers, repair centres, film screenings and often their own fire brigade and fire engine. There's no sign of all this now at Abergavenny; it was all demolished to build townhouses on the grounds. But remnants of the old wall remain, and of course the trees – monkey puzzle and laurels, so beloved of the Victorians. The lodge is now a private home, blue and white curtains at the open windows.

Asylums grew at an astonishing pace in the eighteenth century, becoming considered the 'right place' for people of difference. By 1848 it was compulsory for all counties in Wales and England to build what were termed lunatic asylums. By mid-century, 120 asylums across Wales and England housed 100,000 people. A historian later called them 'museums for the collection of the unwanted'. Somewhere there is a burial ground at the Abergavenny asylum, with 3,500 pauper graves and a single memorial stone. I can't find it during any of my visits.

This growth in inmates caused a commensurate loss of disabled and mentally ill people from their communities. Such is the long shadow of the eighteenth century that this institutionalisation still has an impact today; people often tell me I'm the only disabled person they've ever worked with. For those in generations above me, when they were at school, at university, beginning their careers, people like me were still in institutions. Where would they have met or seen us? For many people, I'm still a curiosity.

I have been absent, too, from the landscape of much of my own life. I became seriously ill at eighteen. I was bedbound for a year, then housebound for much of my twenties.

As a visibly disabled woman, I am often at risk when out

alone, particularly when I seek green space. Being alone in the wood comes with risk as well as relief. People seem to experience an overwhelming sense of ownership over my body. They grab me, satisfying their curiosity, or manhandle me under the guise of being helpful. But strangers forcibly 'helping' me up a slope has damaged my wheelchair and painfully dislocated my joints. I'm penned in by invisible barriers: the stares, the intrusive questions, the unwanted touching, the accusations and all the actions that fall under the term 'hate crimes'.

'What's wrong with you? I hope you don't mind me asking. But is there... hope?' These are questions I am asked often when out in public. I don't want to explain the complex interweaving of my diagnoses, the context of hope in genetic conditions while I'm just trying to get some air. What hope looks like for me is very different to what the questioner may have imagined. My hope is living well with illness and living a life that matters to me. It's not linked to my feet or how well they move. But framing the landscape of these feelings for a stranger isn't how I want to spend my outside time. I have to be polite, as belligerence risks retribution. A person who feels they have the right to ask questions about my body may also react violently when I don't answer and deny what they see as their due. There's another reason I like open spaces: I can see people coming from far away. All this means that I value the sanctuary of space at Abergavenny all the more. When I am here, I feel my breathing soften. That's precious, especially in a pandemic year when I feared for my breath.

Before the asylum was closed, the policy of deinstitutional-isation, of moving treatment and care out of large centres and into the community, was already well underway. A shift towards recognising human rights and listening to service users contributed to the critique of large institutions. The development of psychiatry and social science addressed the harm done in, and by, these institutions. A series of scandals in the 1970s, including one at a Cardiff psychiatric institution, brought public recognition of the brutal and inhumane treatments and living conditions there, which contributed to the calls for their closure. It has been said that this abandonment of asylums represented the most radical physical change in our landscape since the dissolution of the monasteries in the sixteenth century. As early as 1962 the Minister for Health had declared institutions to be relics. Over the following decades inpatient beds declined from 150,000 to 27,000. Major institutionalisation of people with mental health conditions has a surprisingly brief history of only 150 years, but it has left a long shadow.

Where services are available and sufficient, most patients benefit from living in their community. However, asylums provided occupations and other opportunities for social interaction that were not always replicated on the outside. People want connection, care and meaning. For some asylum residents, connection with a community of other patients provided that, but for many others the costs of denied agency and liberty were too great.

I am both glad of the calm I find at Abergavenny Asylum and wish I didn't feel the need to haunt these grounds for safe green space. My disabled body is judged, as are the bodies of my loved ones; my partner who is a person of colour, my transgender and queer community. We struggle to access 'neutral' green space, because our bodies are not considered neutral. My presence and access to these spaces is contested. Abergavenny offers asylum for me as there's space for me here. I have the liberty to come and go. I question why I'm sitting in an old asylum grounds, instead of sitting reading in one of the town's many parks. I don't want to live my life on the edges, at the margins. My difference is indelible; I can't stop being disabled, yet I can seek places that increase my comfort level. Instead of feeling pushed to the margins, I can acknowledge my choice in visiting a place I feel in community with. I feel that here.

I'm sitting in one of the thoughtfully provided shelters. They are wooden, octagonal and Victorian in style. White-painted lacy gingerbread eaves edge the fluted copper roofs, now a verdigris patina. They remind me of the edging on an old train station. Inside, white benches line half-panelled, window-topped dividers. The shelters themselves give cover from the elements but also from being viewed. I'm grateful to access the solace and solitude of nature here, in the spacious breaths of long green lawns and ancient trees. Spying violets, a spider crawling up my sleeve, scatterings of pinecones on the path before me, seeing the chestnuts come into bloom. I value these so much; I kept seeking them, and I found them here. I won't be locked up – not in my home, not in an institution, not in other people's limiting judgements. I am part of this place, this land, made of the same carbon as the trees and the minerals in the earth.

Sitting once again in a shelter, taking in the space today, I feel myself here. I can see the trees, feel the cool breeze that nips with a foretaste of autumn. I am here beyond the boundaries. I sit in my wheelchair under the shelter and watch the birds, the grass blowing in the breeze, the sun moving across the fading sandstone walls. In Abergavenny, in a ghost asylum, I have found a space – I am here.

FAISAL ALI

From the Desert to the Docks and Back

It was the summer of 2007; the first iPhone had just been released, Britney Spears had checked herself into rehab and the fifth Harry Potter movie was out. I was an inquisitive teenager living in London, and it felt like my generation was on the threshold of an exciting, digitally saturated era. But just as the world seemed to be coming within reach of my fidgety fingers, my family was planning something entirely different: I was to be taken for my first visit to our fabled home in a small town in north Somalia called Las Anod. We'd spent weeks packing all the stuff our family in Somalia had asked for, and also what we'd need ourselves. I hadn't the slightest clue what to take. I'd call and ask my cousins if a PlayStation would be useful, or maybe board games, or what kinds of clothes we'd need. Thankfully my mother was on hand, and having grown up in Somalia she was able to put me right. I felt discomforted by my sheer ignorance of a place I was repeatedly informed was our family's 'real' home. It probably wasn't deliberate on the part of my parents, but implicit in the framing of our journey's *raison d'être* was that the UK wasn't *really* home. We were actually from somewhere else, and the time had come to see it.

One of my UK-based cousins, who had visited before, saw

my ignorance as an opportunity for a practical joke. The picture he painted gave me the impression that Somalia would be like a cross between *Black Hawk Down* and a David Attenborough documentary. Other than *Black Hawk Down*, which my father disliked because of the way it glorified American militarism, I'd never even seen any images of Somalia. I looked at the country on maps as a child, interrogating it for hours – its cities, villages, lakes, rivers and roads. Unaware of the vicissitudes of history, war and migration I'd often thought about how arbitrary maps and borders are. Why was Somalia not in South America, for example? Who decided what size it should be, or what shape? Somalia looked like a thick number 7 drawn by the hand of a calligrapher, hanging like a perfectly placed jigsaw piece on the furthest extremity of the Horn of Africa, between the highlands of Ethiopia and the Indian Ocean. I'd come to know Somalia quite well in theory, but it always remained something without a sensory component; intangible, unseen, unsmelt, unheard. Thus my imagination was all I had, fed by my cousin's accounts.

'Our house is huge,' he said. 'We have a massive courtyard, with a hill behind, but apparently if you go out in the evenings there's a woman who will take you away and eat you.' I later learned that this woman was Dhegdheer, a cannibalistic widow of Somali folklore, summoned by parents to scare disobedient children. On the eve of our visit, though I realised Dhegdheer was a myth, Somalia remained for me an exotic place, but I was sure I wouldn't be let down by the reality of it. In truth I already loved something about the country; life there sounded like a movie compared to the familiarity of life in the UK, and I romanticised it as a place of total freedom. A lot of my friends had also been and shared their stories, explaining how they'd learned to speak Somali properly there and strengthened their appreciation and understanding of our culture. It was now my turn to complete a ritual which would help fill that missing part of me. When the day finally arrived, I was itching to go.

After changing in Dubai, we finally boarded the flight to the northern coastal city of Berbera. The seats vibrated violently the whole way on that rickety plane, and I clutched the arm rests tightly. My cousin, who'd visited before, continued to taunt me. 'I hope we make it,' he said with a menacing grin. He knew we would, but I hadn't flown often in my life and I was sure it wasn't meant to be like this. Then at last we were flying over Somalia itself. I recall the awe I felt as I peered out the window, watching the thin slow waves of the clear aquamarine ocean wash up against the faded copper shores of Somalia's northern coast. The contrast was astonishing: land so dry that it looked burned being gently stroked by this vast body of water. The moment I'd been waiting for had arrived. I'd finally returned home to a foreign country.

***

During the last century my family had moved many times between the place we now call Somalia and the United Kingdom. Back then, the territories where Somalis lived in East Africa were mostly divided between the UK and Italy. My maternal grandfather told us that his father arrived in Cardiff around 1908, where he'd go on to become a sailor. In that era shipping was being transformed, as sails gave way to modern coal-powered ships. Working in the engine rooms was difficult and uncomfortable, and the Cardiff locals apparently weren't keen. More labour was needed, so Britain turned to her empire to fill the manpower shortage. My great-grandfather was among those early migrants who settled in the port cities and quickly established cosmopolitan communities of mostly transitory workers. Tiger Bay, Cardiff, was then one of the most important ports in the world. With the influx of foreign labour Cardiff became a microcosm displaying the diversity of the empire. Somalis, Egyptians, Yemenis, Jamaicans, Cypriots, Punjabis and others quickly gave Cardiff a unique feel – simultaneously multicultural and urbane, but still working class. Welsh cosmopolitanism is how I like to think of it – the unique way that we in Wales localised the world. These communities didn't just coexist, but also befriended one another and often intermarried.

The initial welcome wasn't always warm, however. There were frequent riots and demonstrations against the newcomers. Not one to sit around, my great-grandfather led counter-protests. He even met and attended a demonstration alongside the legendary American musician, athlete and activist Paul Robeson, and befriended Sylvia Pankhurst. Cardiff became home, and he married Prudence Maden Dowdry, our great-grandma, who was Irish-Brazilian. They had three children, one of whom, Ibrahim, became our grandfather. They lived together in Tiger Bay – where I also grew up – and my conversations with my grandfather revealed his deep love for the area. I would often listen to his stories of the local dance hall he'd attended, his days as a musician playing the harmonica with his band, his passion for football and rugby and his descriptions of what Tiger Bay used to look like back then.

Grandfather's connection to Cardiff was deep, and on his Merchant Navy identity card, in the space for 'other names', he tellingly wrote 'Native of Cardiff'. Through his often vividly recalled stories I was able to transport myself back in time, and inherit his memories as my heirloom. Not only that, but his stories also changed my own relationship with Cardiff and my view of myself. The experiences he narrated helped me piece together the city's history and the radical changes that had happened during his life, and between his times and those of my own generation. His history was my history; every time I meandered around Loundoun Square or loitered around town, I knew that he'd probably done so thousands of times himself, albeit in a different townscape and among different people. We had living roots in this place, and those roots were something that I shared with him.

His father, Dualeh Aftaag, was never quite settled in Cardiff though. I think he enjoyed adventure and travel too much – why would he have become a sailor and moved to a faraway country otherwise? But he had at least one more motivation for eventually returning to Somalia. Cardiff, and the UK's other port cities, nurtured the nascent Somali nationalist movement. A dedicated anti-colonial nationalist himself, my great-grandfather spent years campaigning with the Somali Youth League, a movement of young Somalis determined to liberate their country from European rule – of which he led the UK chapter. They finally realised their goal in 1960. It was time for him to go home to an independent country which was his, and in early June that year he left. We found notes from the final meeting he convened at Noor Mosque, where he bade farewell to his friends, probably not expecting that his descendants would one day return to Cardiff. I often imagine him taking that ship back home, for the first time in decades, no longer a subject of Her Majesty's government, and what it must have meant to him to see the fruition of a big part of his life's work. He wrote a solemn poem dedicated to Somalia's flag raising, the title of which speaks for itself: 'I am Born Today'.

After a lifetime of travelling, my great-grandfather finally settled down, but his decision to take his sons with him would later prove fateful. As he healed the wound caused by his own dislocation, they would now experience something of what it was like to live away from the place where they'd grown up. It was my grandfather's first trip 'home', but unlike me he was an adult when he first went to Somalia. He would have been very settled in his ways, clear about his tastes and nowhere near as gullible about where he was going. He'd also returned from duty in the Second World War, where he fought in Europe against the Nazis, and probably wasn't too excited about the prospect of settling down in post-war Britain. Perhaps he was drawn by the idea of a slow and peaceful life that might help him forget about the war. Maybe he just wanted to go with his father, or thought of the idea of a sojourn in Somalia as novel and exciting.

***

We landed in Berbera, on the northern coast of Somaliland, where my great-grandfather had departed from almost exactly a century earlier. The airport was small, with just enough space for the plane to land, people to be processed and luggage to be distributed. As I walked down the plane steps the heat was thick and suffocating, and the powerful winds did little to offset its effects. It was the kind of heat that makes the air feel denser, every movement of your limbs that bit more energy consuming. As we left the airport a convoy of drivers was waiting for us outside.

Berbera's landscape wasn't so different from other parts of Somalia: semi-arid and lifeless, with little vegetation save for occasional shrubs. The sky was vast, unbroken by tall buildings. In the day it was a brilliant blue, with the sun shining a molten yellow and light clouds passing quickly with the powerful winds. By night the same sky was a deep black without the ubiquity of urban light pollution that creates a veil between man and the heavens, revealing a sky scattered with more stars than I'd ever seen. When we arrived in Berbera at midday it seemed almost deserted. Only rarely would you see one or two people, sitting outside huts made of corrugated steel from which they'd sell everything from SIM cards to cigarettes, soda and tea. The temperature in Berbera frequently tops 35 degrees, and my father explained that the parched city tucks itself away to sleep from high noon to the late afternoon prayer to avoid the heat.

Beyond the main roads, dirt tracks between houses created an informal road network that kept the city's arteries connected to less accessible places on the fringes. Infrequent trees along the rubble-lined roads provided respite from the heat for goats and stray cats and dogs. Decaying relics of the nineteenth-century Ottoman presence were everywhere apparent. Olive-pistachio-coloured limestone villas with arched doorways and the fading paint of old bleached mosques could be seen across the city. A few buildings had an almost Mediterranean feel, with carved patterns above their windows' colourful wooden frames. They were only missing the climbing vines and hot pink Bougainvillea sprouts. The city's long history was apparent in the architecture and also in a certain languorous vibe, making Berbera feel like a tired but effortlessly beautiful place, trapped between neglect, indifference and the quickly changing fortunes of a country caught between the shifting tides of history.

We continued to Las Anod. The road wasn't great, so we drove slowly, giving me the opportunity to watch the landscape. When the driver wasn't careful, deep potholes would keep us awake. Though the journey was long, it was too much of a novelty ever to bore us. We were driving through Somaliland and north Somalia, windows down, music playing, in an old Toyota Mark II Cressida Wagon, a sturdy and angular 1980s vehicle which felt simultaneously like it could break down at any moment, yet also survive a plunge off the Grand Canyon. Almost everyone was driving one. There wasn't much to see but I was glued to the window, mustering my less than adequate Somali to ask: 'Will we see any animals? What's this place called? How come there's no one around?' And the legendary 'Are we there yet?' The road was narrow, and every time another car passed by we'd have to slow down drastically, almost edging off the road.

Along the route were villages where refreshments were sold. In the larger places you'd often find a tent restaurant with small wooden stools or plastic garden chairs, selling boiled goat or camel meat and white rice, served with tea, camel milk and a small slab of fat. There was always a mosque, not elegant but practical and built for purpose; a large, single-storey building with flaking white pastel paint and a slim minaret. The houses were simple and designed for weather patterns which rarely change: rectangular concrete huts with colourful iron rather than glass windows, usually painted a dim blue or tired red, often with a strip of dark blue paint across the bottom. We continued past these villages along the seemingly never-ending road.

Roadblocks punctuated our journey, giving us an opportunity to chat with people. Sometimes the tone was cordial, even jovial, but at others it was far more serious. Young men, whether legitimate local authorities or armed civilians, would create barriers with thick branches or chains strung between trees, where they'd sit all day waiting for people to stop so they could charge to use the road. It wasn't always necessary to pay, but given the dire economic situation out there I figured my father and our drivers didn't mind passing a few shillings to them. 'This is an awfully thin stack,' one young man told my father in a village just outside the city of Burao. 'Let me fatten that up', he responded, 'That should be extra tea and maybe some cigarettes.' I asked my father to show me the banknotes. They were blue or brown, tattered and torn, with Arabic and Somali inscriptions issued in the name of a central bank which no longer existed. The denominations were also huge. My father indifferently handed me a 1000 Somali shilling note, which I soon discovered was barely enough to buy a coke.

The Somali shilling is perhaps a metaphor for the Somali nation as a whole. When the government collapsed in 1991 one would have imagined that the shilling would disappear with it, but just like the Somali people the currency has endured, and

Somalis continue to use it as a means of exchange. Similarly, although state authority was then negligible, Somalis found innovative ways to muddle through, erecting fragile regional governments but mainly relying on other organic social institutions to maintain social harmony, like religion and the clan and family groups which had grown in importance in the absence of the Somali state.

Clans are especially important, and learning about how they work led me to the uncomfortable discovery that, if I follow the patrilineal Somali naming tradition, my surname isn't actually Ali. Every newborn takes a personal name, his father's name as his middle, and then his father's after that, and so on going back generations. These names often link back to particular villages or regions from which a family hails, and create wide networks of mutual obligation which act as an insurance policy against violence and financial misfortune. This patrilineal clan system allows Somalis to quickly identify relatives who they are obliged to protect, support and vouch for when needed. The absence of the Somali state for the last two decades strengthened this organic institution, and during one outing I got a clear idea of how it worked. Sitting in the shade of a large acacia tree outside Las Anod, elders from my clan deliberated on the compensation owed to another clan when a member of ours took another man's life. It's common not to know the man or woman whom the clan is gathering to support, as some clans are very large. The money of course doesn't make up for the loss of a life, but is meant both as a gesture and a support for the family who could fall into poverty if a bread-winner is killed. This system protects a delicate balance in places lacking other systems of dispute resolution. These obligations are activated at the age of adulthood, and I was very recently expected, alongside my brothers, to contribute to another similar case.

**

At the time of my first visit, Somalia had been without a central government for over fifteen years, and, without romanticising the era before, the country had certainly changed from how it had been prior to the war. At first, my grandfather had been delighted by the choice to move to Somalia. The country was young, dynamic, democratic. It had won plaudits across Africa, with Kenneth Kaunda declaring that 'Somali democracy should be a model for other African countries'. Like most African nations emerging from the asphyxiating chokehold of colonial rule, Somalia was in dire need of skilled labour, and my grandfather quickly found work as an electrician in the northern city of Hargeisa, where he'd marry Ebado Istahil and father my mother, my uncles and my aunts. He was short and stocky, well poised and always clean shaven, with a neat combover. Though I only knew him in his old age he was a thoughtful, observant but very direct man, with the energy of a meerkat and a thick and coarse Cardiff accent. He had small deep-set eyes which would subtly study anything within his view before he spoke, full cheeks and a strong jawbone. He'd end up spending over two decades in Somalia, and even remained after his father passed away, but Somalia was a turbulent place during the Cold War, struggling like many postcolonial African states with challenges of identity and the centrifugal forces of global politics.

For years he'd continued his life as an electrician, solving the practical problems that accompanied providing electricity to the city for the first time. His Somali was strong, and he had a broad vocabulary, but even in his later years the Cardiff accent coloured the way he used the language; the throaty sounds of the Somali language often came out flatter, and the vowels were extended in a manner more common in Tiger Bay. 'Hang on' would become his nickname among the thousands of people he reconnected to the grid. But following the failed 1977 Ogaden War with Ethiopia the writing was on the wall for Somalia. Things slowly began falling apart, and the regime steadily became more repressive. Major projects would still take place, students would go to school and one of my uncles, in high school at the time, would describe those years as some of his best. But the Somali state was rotting from within, and my grandfather knew it.

In the mid-eighties he returned to Cardiff to get everything set for our family so they could slowly begin making their way there. For him it was a return to a life he'd once known, despite the huge changes in Cardiff during his absence. He settled down again in Tiger Bay, which had since been renamed Butetown. For my mother, uncles and aunts, it was the first time they'd left Somalia to 'return' to a home they'd never known. But there wasn't much choice, because while the previous migrations of our family were driven by economic motives, this time they were fleeing for their lives. My mother related stories of the hateful graffiti painted on their house, and the dead bodies her younger brothers would encounter on their morning walks to school. By the early nineties our whole family had relocated. Our great-grandfather had moved to Cardiff in pursuit of fortune and adventure in the early 1900s; almost a century later we'd returned in search of a safe haven from war, and so another generation of children would be born and raised in Cardiff. When things settled down in the early 2000s, some of my family members made a short return. My uncle couldn't travel to Mogadishu, which was the last place he'd lived, because it was still volatile, so that was how Las Anod became our home base. Now he just had to sell it to us.

Eventually a village appeared on the horizon, and our driver pointed it out. 'We've almost arrived,' he said, and I leaped up. The gates of Las Anod were two unconnected white walls on either side of the road, emblazoned with the Somali flag, a large blue stallion and some advertisements for local telecom companies. Here was another checkpoint, but we got through very quickly because our drivers were locals in the city, who the guards recognised.

***

Las Anod rests in the womb of several faded beige limestone hills that act as a kind of natural barrier cosily cocooning the town. Nowadays they bristle with phone masts, but they were once used as watch-posts to defend the town from hostile incursions. One of these hills, Sayyid's Mountain, is named after one of Las Anod's most famous adopted sons. Sayyid Mohammed Abdullah Hassan was renowned and at times infamous outside Somalia for his determined resistance to the British colonialists. His inexhaustible enmity earned him the moniker 'The Mad Mullah' in the British press. Hassan mobilised fighters from Las Anod and across north Somalia to build a multi-clan mystical religious movement which at its peak created a state that encompassed a large part of modern northeast Somalia. Following his death, the movement collapsed and colonial rule was consolidated, but his efforts established him as a hero for many Somalis.

Around Las Anod, Hassan still has iconic status. Many of his most dedicated fighters came from here, and it was an important base for his operations in his campaigns against the Brits and Italians. Even though Hassan himself often acknowledged that there wasn't necessarily much to fight for – Somalia was underdeveloped and poor after all – it was the principle which was at stake. An accomplished poet, in one of his verses Hassan wrote, 'I have no forts, no houses... I have no cultivated fields, no silver or gold for you to take... All you can get from me is war.' It was this hard-nosed attitude that won him plaudits across Somalia.

I still remember how excited I was the first time we climbed Sayyid's Mountain. Steep and rock-strewn, the path can be dangerous at times, especially when powerful winds blow higher up. Each footstep requires care. A fall wouldn't spell death unless you were really unlucky, but you'd probably require more medical attention than Las Anod could offer. As the sun sank in a cool red glow, electric crackles rattled the mosque speakers below, and then an ensemble of staggered and wistful calls to pray rose up like a wave gathering strength to their crescendo – *Allahu Akbar*, *Allahu Akbar* – before their tranquil descent washed softly over the city as the muezzin's voice petered out, its echo whispering faintly between the mountains: *La Ilaha Illallah*.

This mountain, a faithful watchman for Las Anod, was named after Sayyid because of his struggle with such meagre resources against a formidable and overwhelming foe. Though he was maligned in the British press, locals here cling to his legacy, with the clans of this region viewing their participation in those battles as a point of pride. In a society which keeps track of names patrilineally, developing into large clans which trace their fathers back thousands of years, it's significant that when people don't refer to themselves by their clan names, they often call themselves Dervishes, named after the fighting core loyal to Sayyid Abdullah that entered the world stage and crossed swords with a global empire.

***

One morning we were loaded into cars heading out of the city to what Somalis call the *miyi* (pronounced me-yee). In England this might be thought of as the 'countryside', but that word has connotations that don't reflect the Somali reality. You can't call it camping or compare it to an English village. The miyi means the bush, the outback, places with little to no development and where life is fluid and organised around a different economic principle and a different kind of society. Miyi also carries a second, deeper meaning, harking back to the pre-urban nomadic lives Somalis lived before mass migration into the cities shortly after independence.

I was still groggy from being woken when we set off. The terrain seemed entirely without landmarks, but when I asked my father how they knew where we were going, he responded 'Me and these boys know every rock, mountain and bush of this land'. We sped through a huge, dusty plain in our Toyota pickup; everything was a lacklustre, lifeless orange colour from the dust that rested on the scorched land. To our left we saw a tree with baboons hanging gently and frolicking in the late morning sun.

We eventually arrived and parked the truck next to a large tree, and within no time my uncles and father began digging a large well, and had put up a tent. My brothers, cousins and I looked around. Nothing but desert to the horizon, and beyond that probably some more. 'What do you think?' my mother asked sarcastically, aware that I'd probably whine her into a coma if she let me. I went for a walk with one of my cousins, and by the time we'd returned, two large wells had been dug and filled with water for drinking and washing. For two weeks we'd have an opportunity to live like our ancestors, directly facing the elements, albeit with a few more amenities. I could live without a bed or roof it seemed, but not without ketchup and a Snickers bar. If you walked for about an hour there was a hamlet where you might be able to find sweets and other conveniences, although they didn't last long.

Our paternal grandfather used to graze his livestock in these territories, and though the location initially seemed arbitrary to me, we'd actually made camp right next to his mobile home. He hadn't abandoned his nomadic lifestyle, and had spent almost his entire life in these open spaces with his wife and children. He had dozens of goats and camels with whom he lived symbiotically; he found them vegetation to graze and oases to drink from, and they provided milk and meat to both eat and sell. This mutual dependence was the cornerstone of pre-urban life for many Somalis. The goats were small, white, restless and noisy. I don't think they ever stopped bleating unless they were asleep. We'd spend mornings playing with them and milking them.

***

My father told me that my grandfather's experience of living in the miyi gave him mental toughness. This was something my father wanted to impart to us, but he also wanted to show us how much our family had changed in a generation. Our paternal grandfather was a pastoral nomad; he had his animals, his shirt, a long colourful cotton loincloth which he wrapped around his waist, his sandals, a tent which he'd erect wherever he found sustenance, and a fiercely independent attitude.

Our maternal grandfather was something of a nomad himself, but of quite a different fashion, having been born and raised in Cardiff, an important city in the world's most powerful industrial empire. The two branches of our family were now face to face, and the impact of migration meant in truth we no longer totally recognised each other. Our branch had broken its natural rhythm, but this journey brought us back to it, reconnecting us, not just with our family, but also with nature. One night we sat in the moonlight, gazing awestruck at the stars, and as we became more confident and started sleeping outside we would watch the night sky pass through its phases, and study the various stars and constellations. It became hard to ignore the fact that we are a lonely species clinging to a rock hurtling through space. I was reminded of a verse from the Quran in which humanity is tauntingly asked 'Are ye the harder to create, or is the heaven that He built?'

Within a few days we adapted to the new normal. Our cousins, who had lived as nomads their whole lives, were different in their manners and attitudes. They were less fussy, unimpressed by the things we were impressed by, and often made no requests of the passers-by on the route back into the nearby towns for things to bring back. I'd describe their attitude as one of soft resignation to the vagaries of fate, but that wouldn't be quite right. They were more aware of the little control we actually have, able to manage their appetites and adapt quickly to new requirements, taking charge of what they could. We were more brittle and needy, and required more comfort.

The nomadic lifestyle demands that families work together as intergenerational units, passing down knowledge, sharing duties and relying on the larger clan where necessary to ensure any problems can be collectively resolved. We weren't excluded from this. Even though my family had left home we found new ways to be of use. Our parents often sent money back, like many other Somalis in the diaspora. This money was for the wells and other necessities for life. We tracked down medicines for our relatives, and provided any other support where needed. Meanwhile, they maintained a tradition which went back generations. Years later, my father told me that the place where we'd camped had itself developed into a small site due to the wells we'd dug, and so had entered local history. That small expedition, and what was left of it, would support others during their journeys criss-crossing the desert. Visitors call the place 'Camp Abdulaziz', after my father's name, and remark that this is the location where a man from abroad once brought his whole family to give them an experience of what it's like to live out here. We now had our own local legend.

But though the miyi was the preface to our family's story, there was a chasm between the way the diasporic part of our family understood the concept of home, and the way our immediate relatives who we'd left behind understood it. For the former it was fluid and mobile, constructed where fortune favoured and livestock could graze. In the UK we had addresses to which we could always return, places where we could expect to encounter familiar people – the family, friends and acquaintances whose reliable presence colours a place with a certain intimacy. It was momentarily unsettling to realise that this journey of self-discovery didn't mesh with my newly inherited understanding of home as a fixed place.

Looked at differently, though, were the lives of my family's two branches really so different? Weren't we also nomads of a kind? My great-grandfather's sense of adventure had launched us on a much more ambitious journey, crossing continents multiple times in search of our own greener pastures, winging it somewhat every step of the way. True, the miyi was our patrimony, but this knowledge was freeing rather than limiting; if home is nowhere, it can also be anywhere.

SOPHIE BUCHAILLARD

Revolving Doors

A jackdaw's hard repetitive 'tchack' cuts through the clattering wings of the pigeons standing sentinel on our rooftop. They await the seeds an elderly neighbour scatters on her birdfeeder each day at 6am. Then the heavy birds take flight – my cue to get up also.

'Do you think we'll be able to hear bird songs when we move to Penarth?' I once asked my late husband, who met the question with an amused smile.

The flat is on the top floor, surrounded by trees, like an island amid a sea of green canopies. From here, the low murmur of urban life seems muted, made less relevant by the chromatic passage of the seasons and the routines of woodpeckers, blue tits, bats and squirrels; quite a contrast with a Parisian childhood that was marked by the revving of the number 22 bus passing every twelve minutes along the avenue below. Each morning at six I woke to the high-pitched screech of the municipal bin lorry's lifting mechanism as it tilted the regiments of wheelie bins that stood in front of the large Haussmanien buildings. I heard the concierge swearing as he dragged the bins back through the service entrance, hard plastic thudding against the paved alleyway, the clanking of keys absorbed by the reinforced steel door which he shut behind him. I would rise then, knowing my mother would have been preparing breakfast while my father shaved, filling the apartment with the smell of sandalwood, freshly baked bread and ground coffee.

Today, my son and I are travelling back in time, catching the Penarth train to Cardiff Central, on to the London train to Paddington, and from there to St Pancras International where the Eurostar will carry us to Paris. A twelve-hour journey from Wales to Paris, a recreation in reverse of one I took twenty years ago, when I'd flown from Charles de Gaulle to Cardiff International Airport. The date was the 14th of September 2001, three days after the catastrophic event which continues to impact the way we travel. Today's trip is a long overdue pilgrimage to show my son his French roots, a trip delayed by the passing of his father and the many questions that came after grief, about where we belong, now that he is no longer with us.

I lay down two plates on the kitchen counter, pour us breakfast tea with a splash of milk, and butter two slices of bread before drowning them in Marmite. In the background, the radio is reporting the advance of the Taliban towards Kabul, while the American troops who occupied Afghanistan after 9/11 execute presidential orders to depart. The date has a particular meaning for me, one that marks the start of an accidental migration from which I am only returning now.

My son emerges from his bedroom fully dressed, eager for the adventure to begin. We eat our toast and drink our brew hurriedly, grab our bags and lock the front door without as much as a glance back. 'I bought this suitcase when I first moved to Cardiff,' I tell him, lifting a wheeled blue case and carrying it down the stairs. 'We've been everywhere together.' I place my charge onto the ground outside and gently pat it like you might a faithful companion. My son rolls his eyes at the sentimental display, then volunteers to pull the beast to the station.

The pavement around our place is distorted by tree roots. The case hits every ridge and crack, rumbling loudly, sending spooked jackdaws into flight: one, ten, thirty, like a procession, all the way to Penarth station. There, only one track remains from the vibrant network of the Industrial Revolution, the quarry since flooded to make way for Cosmeston lake and country park in 1978, the year of my birth. A mould-green two-coach Arriva train rests on the track, an old relic that would have been replaced as part of the electrification of the line, on reprieve because of the delays caused by the pandemic. I hand my son his mask and we both step into an empty carriage, faces covered, looking like bandits. Earlier, a train operator interviewed on the radio had lamented that only sixty per cent of passengers have returned. It's a step back for sustainable travel, although on every news outlet the climate crisis has been overshadowed by daily counts: of new positive tests, new patients in intensive care, new deaths. Within a week, the news will be reporting more figures: 20,000 refugees over three years, airlifted to the UK from Kabul airport, supported by armed eighteen-year-old soldiers juggling guns with babies.

At Cardiff Central, the London train is thirty minutes late. We sit and stare at the station clock, desperate for no further delays.

'Will we make it?' my son asks, leaning into my shoulder.

'I think so,' I reply, my voice muffled by folds of cotton. I count the spare minutes on my fingers over and over again, as if doing so could somehow bend time. I hear my mother's voice telling me that we should have flown instead. The tannoy comes to life, apologising for a further thirty-five-minute delay.

'Will we make it now?'

'I don't know,' I say, my reply this time absorbed by a distorted platform announcement in Welsh then repeated in English. I feel the weight of doubt pressing against my chest. Maybe this journey is a silly indulgence? What my family always assumed to be temporary morphed into a husband, a mortgage, a child. Over time, what we had started to look like a life. Strangers always asked, 'why Wales?', bemused to hear I had left Paris behind. I met someone, I would say, and they would nod, because of course, love explains everything. 'Except you left us,' I murmur.

'What did you say?'

'The London train is always late,' I tell my son. 'We'll be alright.'

We could have flown. We used to. My mother worked as a long-haul flight hostess for Avianca throughout the sixties and seventies, dressed in impeccably tailored uniforms, hair pinned into a high bun under a red felted hat, lipstick to match, high heels. Bogotá to Miami, Miami to Paris, Paris to Melbourne. Part of an army of glamorous women serving the capitalist dream on hard plastic trays to grey-suited men hungry for growth, like an all-you-can-eat buffet. Thanks to her position, our family benefited from free plane tickets that allowed us to cross continents with ease. We flew often. By the time I was the age my son is now, I had visited the red stone cathedrals of the Grand Canyon, sand arches carved by the wind near Lake Placid, the white terraces of the medina at Fes, the intricate architecture of Aya Sophia and the dry plains of Maasai Mara, inhabited by big cats and Maasai warriors, their ear lobes stretched by plastic film cannisters. *Jambo*!

We might have flown from Cardiff.

'It's only an hour flight,' my mother had said on the phone.

'Think of your grandson's future,' I'd replied.

So now we wait, for the Swansea train to arrive and carry us to London, for the Hammersmith and City line to transport us to the Eurostar departure lounge, for the border patrols to confirm we have the right documentation to clear customs: a sworn statement for the French government to confirm we are symptom-free, proof of vaccination for me, a negative test of less than twenty-four hours for my son. The officer behind the glass panel orders us to remove our masks so he can confirm our identities. The image of a veiled woman uncovering her face at Amsterdam airport many years ago flashes through my mind, chased by the piercing blue eyes of an Afghan girl captured in 1984 by Steve McCurry for the cover of *National Geographic* – a haunting gaze that remained on the wall of my childhood bedroom until I left Paris.

I'm pulled back by the heavy thump of the French official stamping our passports.

'Look, you've got a stamp!' I show it to my son, trying to sound jovial.

Inwardly, I cringe at the first concrete sign of what until now has been an abstract change. The open door that brought me to Wales has shut. It is with black passports that we return.

At Paris-Gare du Nord the tall caryatids in white stone monitor our arrival. My mother is standing on the main concourse, straight as a marble statue, face hidden behind a surgical mask. We huddle, unsure whether to hug after months of social isolation.

'I brought the car,' she says, dragging her grandson by the hand. I try to keep up, yanking the blue suitcase behind me. I'm no longer aware of the noise the case makes amid the din of city traffic. Looking ahead I notice, just before they disappear into the car, that my mother and son are the same height.

Soon we reach the Opera Garnier, a work commissioned by Napoleon III in his own honour and filled with the technical innovations of the time. A few minutes later, the church of La Madeleine, originally built to commemorate Napoleon's great army, stands before us, its colonnades encased in scaffolding. Then we're alongside the golden-tipped obelisk that's proudly anchored in the middle of the Place de la Concorde. To our right, the Champs-Elysées, lined by rows of imposing horse-chestnut trees, shrink towards the Arc de Triomphe and the flame of the Unknown Soldier. To our left is the Orangery, a small, glass-panelled museum flanked by the Seine and the Rue de Rivoli. My mother and I point out these familiar buildings to my son, as I realise for the first time how many of the capital's tourist landmarks are linked to France's military history. Ahead of us, across the river, I gesture towards the National Assembly.

'It looks like a Greek temple!' he exclaims, as I recall an anecdote about the statues in front of the Assembly having to be replaced by resin copies in the 1990s, on account of the damage caused by traffic pollution. The next minute, we are driving between the Petit and Grand Palais, two glass and metal buildings temporarily erected for the Universal Exhibition of 1889, which still host large art collections. The Grand Palais to our right is scaffolded too. Ahead of the Olympic Games in three years, my mum explains. Its art collection has been moved to a futuristic-looking tent on the rectangular plane of the Champ de Mars. Everywhere, Paris is fighting to retain its air of grandeur.

Eventually, we reach our destination, an apartment block on the western edge of the city. My mother presses a button and manoeuvres her car between two imposing automatic gates and into an underground carpark.

'It's very dark,' my son remarks, blinking in the automatic lighting which meets us as we descend into darkness.

This is not the place of my childhood. After my father passed, my mother moved to a smaller apartment, one I have never seen. She parks the car and leads us out, through a series of locked doors.

'There is the lift.' She points to a sliding panel. Inside, floor-to-ceiling mirrors fail to relieve the claustrophobia of the little cage. I never liked lifts. But my son is excited by the novelty, and presses every button before my mother and I can object. We ride up like mackerel in a tin, the door opening and closing on each floor.

'It all looks the same,' he says.

He's right. We catch glimpses of corridors painted a peach colour, of doors trimmed in sage-green, of large brass handles. We follow my mother as she steps out onto her floor. Large, tinted mirrors capture the electric light, sending back a warm glow across the marble tiles. Next to each door, a small plaque is etched with the name of its occupant. My mother pulls a key from her handbag and unlocks the second door on the left. I hold my breath as the door opens onto this unknown place – *her* apartment, not the stage of my childhood memories.

Living in a foreign country half of my life, I have often wondered what makes a house a home. As I step into the apartment, I am assailed by smells from childhood – *ras el hanout* from the kitchen, my mother's perfume in the bathroom, the faint scent of cigar emanating from familiar furniture. The apartment is smaller, lighter, laid out differently, but within its walls my mother has recreated our home. Here, each carpet, each table, each chair has a place in my memory. The decorative objects which signify moments from my parents' lives are all around us. Silver Moroccan jewellery from my mother's childhood in Rabat; carved wooden combs from various trips my father took for work in West Africa; a little bronze statue of a running man, bought on a family visit to the Rodin Museum when I was ten. While my mother gives her grandson a tour of the apartment, I sit in the oddly familiar living room as if for the hundredth time. The tightness in my chest has finally lifted.

The day my son was born in Cardiff was the day I started planning this trip. At first, I intended to visit with the newborn, to introduce him to his French family across the sea. In Roath Park where we lived, piles of rust-coloured leaves soon gave way to a heavy cover of snow, the last one of its kind in south Wales. For weeks, parked cars lay buried beneath monticules of frozen snow, consolidated by the city snowploughs pushing fresh falls aside to prioritise ambulance access to the hospital. Our life retreated into a routine of feeds and nappy changes that first year. We would go out only for salutary walks, manoeuvring the pram out of thick puddles of gooey mud and melted snow. Then came the first steps, taken from the rose garden to Roath Lake where we threw handfuls of seed to the swans.

With a child, time takes on a different consistency. Our life became a revolving door between our house and the local nursery, our house and primary school, our house and a growing number of after-school activities. In the meantime, my mother sent news from Paris of my father's slow and steady decline. There is time, I kept thinking. As my son grew, my father seemed to wither in equal measure, yet there never seemed to be a suitable time to visit.

After his passing, my mother embarked on a series of trips of her own, revisiting the places of her youth, chasing remnants of the man who had shared her life for fifty years. In the white walls of the medina in Fes she found a familiarity that was not reflected in the covered faces of the many veiled women.

'It never used to be this way,' she told me on the phone, asking when we would visit.

'I don't have time,' I'd always tell her. I am not sure whether I believed that, or whether I was scared to find I missed my old life.

Then my husband visited the GP surgery for a persistent cough, which ended in a specialist unit at the Heath hospital. The decimated patch of grass beyond the concourse, overshadowed by tall concrete buildings, became our new backyard. It was a place where picnic benches and water features competed with the smell of surgical disinfectant, and where patients in pyjamas and nurses in blue scrubs came to catch a ray of sunshine.

On our second day in Paris we take the bus to the Esplanade du Trocadero, but it is hidden from view by large sheets of opaque plastic behind which builders pressure-wash the stone buildings back to white, while outside street vendors tout miniature replicas of the Eiffel Tower. The real thing stands across the river, its feet hidden by plywood. It's as if the whole of Paris has been wrapped into protective gear, while waves of masked tourists continue to stand in the middle of heavy traffic hoping to catch the ultimate shot.

'I thought we could be visitors for a day,' my mum explains, pointing at an open-top bus decorated with a big vinyl-wrapped tower. We climb the winding staircase and find a seat. A man hands us a pair of cheap earphones.

'It's channel two for English,' he tells me.

For two hours we hop from landmark to landmark. The Invalides first, Napoleon Bonaparte's tomb capped with a majestic golden dome; Notre Dame still bearing the scars from the fire which turned its nave into a gaping hole not so long ago; the Arc de Triomphe, which an artist has gained authorisation to wrap in a giant shroud. Everywhere, tourists marvel at the audio description of buildings hidden behind plastic sheets. It is as if we are too late.

My mother and I call upon our memories to describe the intricacies of each edifice to my son. The blue of the cathedral's stained glass, the Arc statues representing the fallen, the names of battles engraved alongside lists of those who were lost. We tie these to family anecdotes of school visits to the cathedral and a grandfather lost on the battlefield. Together we perform an exercise in oral tradition, a transfer of memory so that my son can graft himself onto this new city.

I journeyed to Wales with a single suitcase, a student grasping the opportunity to free flow around Europe, looking for myself. I returned a mother, widowed by a heavy guillotine, my belonging folded into the face of a ten-year-old boy. What should have been a visit, morphed into a pilgrimage.

By day three my son has adopted the little room adjacent to

the kitchen as his own. On waking, he pulls the blue curtains with Provencal patterns that once decorated my childhood room, opens the window and steps onto the white tiled balcony, inhaling the scent of flowers my mother has planted in large terracotta pots.

'What's that smell?' he asks, when I join him.

I lean towards the red petals, the earthy fragrance filling my nostrils. For a moment, I am back inside a makeshift greenhouse in Morocco.

'Geraniums. They were my grandmother's favourite.' I step back inside. 'Help me set breakfast.'

As we lay the table in the dining room, I consider my mother's choice of flowers. Our childhood memories are olfactive. After my father passed, I sprinkled myself with sandalwood so he would stay with me a little longer. Strangely, I don't associate Wales with any smell, only the sound of birdsongs I could not name in French.

A few more days will pass, memories making way for new routines: my son walking to the bakery each morning to pick up a loaf of bread; our reading sessions on the balcony in the warm afternoon sunshine; several rounds of monopoly at night. I will understand these new markers as signs that my wandering is finally over. Then one day he asks, 'When are we going home?', and I nod, recognising that to him this is just an interlude, our starting points cardinal opposites.

We make our journey in reverse: from Gare du Nord to St Pancras International, from Paddington to Cardiff Central, further along until we reach Penarth. My bones ache from the weight of the voyage. It's like a safety line has broken, my thoughts adrift. The next morning, I wake to the jackdaw's 'tchack', the restless pigeons' wings, the scent of baking bread from the kitchen.

My son opens the bedroom door. 'I made breakfast,' he says. 'Welcome home.'

GIANCARLO GEMIN

The Valleys of Venice:
Memories of an Italian immigrant in Wales

i.m. Elena Gemin (nee Zuanelli) 1929–2020

My mother moved back to Italy permanently in 2008, where she lived in a small apartment in Treviso, which is about thirty minutes by train from Venice, her place of birth. When she was asked how she was settling in her answer was habitually the same: 'I feel lost.' She was emotionally pulled back to Wales, and yet when she had lived in Britain she'd always felt drawn to her native Italy. I remember my father playfully mocking her for welling up at the sight of Venice in a Cornetto advert. Hers was a perpetual state of feeling adrift, and so her answer was to the point: she had lost her sense of homeland, having left Italy at twenty-two, only to return there for her remaining years at seventy-nine years of age. Her story is about the physical and emotional bond made with the country in which you take root – a country whose very recollection could make her misty-eyed after her return to Italy.

She was interviewed for an Exhibition of Italian Memories in Wales in 2010. The interviewer asked about her journey from Venice to Wales, following her fiancé, Giovanni. This was in 1951, and she was travelling alone for the first time.

'Were there other women travelling on their own?'

'No. That I knew of, no. There were others that went but they were accompanied by their brother or someone in the family... No one came on their own... You need guts... which I didn't have at that time.'

One immigrant among the thousands of Italians who settled in south Wales throughout the twentieth century, she had never travelled beyond north-eastern Italy, let alone over the borders into Switzerland and France. Her eyes always narrowed at the memory of her first sight of the Rhondda valley, and the contrast it offered to Venice. The noble, curved domes and pastel-rendered buildings of 'La Serenissima' replaced by the sharp silhouettes and dark-hued industrial buildings; the scalloped, terracotta roof tiles now forbidding black slate. She would pull the word, 'greeey', to emphasise her first impression of that landscape, as well as the new degree of cold, wet weather: '*Freeeddo!*' She came from a place that was surrounded by the verdant, lapping Adriatic lagoon, and now this had been substituted for the small town of Senghenydd, chiselled into the Rhondda valley, where she was to build a life with my father.

Elena Zuanelli was born on Giudecca, a thin strip of land which is part of the Dorsoduro district of Venice. She lived in an apartment block behind the Church of the Redentore, which can be seen on the island of Giudecca as you look across the water from St Mark's square.

'In Venice everyone is on top of each other,' she would say. When you opened the shutters in the morning, you would be close enough to toss a bulb of garlic to the opposite apartment. The washing lines criss-crossed between the buildings, and the linen that flapped in the Adriatic breeze would touch that of your neighbours.

To this day most Venetians have a love-hate relationship with the hordes of year-round sightseers on their front doorstep: necessary for fiscal survival, yet an unrelenting presence. My mother liked the tourists. She once recalled an American woman who spoke very good Italian, telling her how lucky she was to live in 'the most beautiful city in the world'. She would often meet lost travellers in the narrow streets, and they would invariably ask directions for 'Piazza San Marco'. She picked up the English for *'sempre dritto'* (straight on), which always seemed to be the correct direction, no matter where they were in Venice.

Giudecca is a short boat-bus ride across the three hundred metres of the Canale di Giudecca, the busy shipping thoroughfare of Venice. My father, Giovanni, was born in the San Marco district of Venice itself, the youngest of a family of nine. They lived on the Rio Terà degli Assassini (notorious a century or two before for a spate of murders by disguised assassins, which had led to the council providing street lighting and imposing a ban on false beards). His father was a coal merchant, which was an irony as in his mid-twenties Giovanni accepted the invitation of the British National Coal Board to come to Wales and work down the mines of Windsor, Llanbradach and Rockwood. By contrast, my mother's family consisted only of her mother, brother and her father, who was the night watchman of a cotton mill on Giudecca. As a young woman she had dark, striking features, reminiscent of Anna Magnani, although without the ferocity. She told me that her mind had never wandered beyond the Venetian lagoon, an attitude that was perhaps common to many living a village life all over the world. After the war, she was fortunate to get a job as a shop assistant for a photographer near Saint Mark's Square. In 1950 Giovanni entered that photographer's shop and offered her a toasted chestnut, marking the beginning of their courtship. Unfortunately, my grandmother took a dislike to him, and my mother often told the story of, after they were engaged, her mother bumping into an old acquaintance. She mentioned that my mother was being courted by one of the Gemins – the coal merchants.

'Which one of them?' the woman asked with a raised eyebrow.

'The youngest,' my grandmother replied. 'Giovanni.'

The woman's eyes opened wide as if an earthquake was rumbling underfoot. 'Him!' she cried. 'The worst of them!'

It was within a year that my father showed my mother a booklet. On the front cover was a smiling miner, under which was written '*Schema per reclutamento volontario di lavoratori Italiani da impiegarsi nella minere di carbone in sottosuolo in Gran Bretagna*' (voluntary scheme for the recruitment of Italian workers for underground coalmining employment in Great Britain). The booklet, in Italian and English, was in fact a contract, complete with clauses, to be signed at a local agency. Free transport, accommodation and food for the journey was promised, as well as twenty pounds upon arrival; full coalmining training would be provided, together with one safety helmet and a pair of boots. They would have the same rights as British workers and be offered English classes if their spoken English was not of a good enough standard. The wages of one hundred and ten shillings a week, when converted to lira, were enticing. My mother told me that initially she thought my father was only considering it as a last resort; after all, it was one thing to come from a family that sold coal and another altogether to go underground and dig it out – a notoriously dangerous profession. In fact, he had already visited the recruitment agency and decided it was too good an opportunity to turn down, especially when compared to the high unemployment of post-war Italy. Wales was a likely location, as one of the biggest coal producers, though, as far as my mother was concerned, it was a country that could have been on another continent. She recalled that when my father showed her a particular clause in the booklet – 'Volunteers will not be allowed to bring with them dependents or any other relatives' – she burst into tears as she assumed it meant their engagement was off. But the booklet went on to explain that the immigrant miners could subsequently apply for their wives to join them at their own expense. He asked if she would follow him and marry him over there.

In the interview, my mother described the moment she informed her mother of her intention to follow my father to the land of Wales – a country about which she knew nothing other than its shape in an atlas.

'Are you out of your mind?' her mother asked. 'Tell me the truth – did he give you something, a drug of some sort?'

My mother giggled at the recollection, and yet, against her mother's advice, she stuck by her promise to my father, and six months after he had left for Wales she was reluctantly seen off by her mother at Santa Lucia train station on 5 December 1951.

I remember her telling me how alone she felt on the train, when previously she had never travelled further than the Alto

Adige to gaze at the Dolomites. Only seconds after departing Santa Lucia station, she would have travelled across the Ponte della Liberta, the bridge that, as a four-year-old in 1933, she would have seen being constructed under the orders of Mussolini. Now, in 1951, she did not know that she wouldn't cross back over it for another four years, and under circumstances equally uncertain and filled with trepidation.

At the border crossing she remembered hearing German for the first time since the occupation, and having her papers scrutinised. Venice had survived the war relatively unscathed (it was said to have been deliberately spared by the Allies), but as the train passed through the cities of France she saw the devastation the war had caused and the slow rebuilding toward a normal life. She said it seemed to her as if everyone was on the move – either escaping or trying to return home. A post-war migration. She had little money and few provisions for the two-day trip, added to which she endured two sleepless nights. All her life she retained a phobia of crowds, though, conversely, she always loved a train journey: she would stare out of the window at the passing countryside, grinning like a child whenever she caught a glimpse of sheep with lambs. This train was taking her into the unknown and the unfamiliar, her mind *piena de dubbi* (engulfed in doubts). My father had settled in the Rhondda valley, and my mother clutched a letter which explained where she needed to go once she had crossed the English channel.

But first there was the crossing itself, which unfortunately coincided with a storm.

'I thought I was going to die,' she said.

How could waves rise so high, when in Venice they innocently slap at the city's foundations? The *vaporetto* water buses of Venice chug along gently, with the slightest rocking motion, but this angry sea and rolling ship filled her with terror and premonitions of doom: her mother had surely been right – she was paying for her foolhardy decision to disregard her advice and follow Giovanni to Wales. I remember that she would always turn away from the TV screen if there was footage on board a ship: merely looking at that rocking movement would trigger nausea.

She was met at Victoria by a distant friend of my father's family who was living in London. It was her first experience of a metropolis whose smallest borough could swallow Venice whole. She said it was frightening for her to be among the rushing, stony-faced crowds – a gloomy contrast to the happy, strolling tourists of Venice. Then she was on the train to Wales, travelling yet further still from home. When she finally arrived at Cardiff station she was completely drained of energy due to the sleepless nights and the terror of the Channel crossing, not to mention her mother's cold farewell in Venice, still ingrained in her mind. But there was Giovanni and the rain of Wales to greet her.

She had seen nothing like the streets of the Valleys, with their lines of stark, terraced houses. *'Where have I come?'* she said softly in the interview. She could stand in one street and look down onto the one below or up to the street above; she was back to living on top of her neighbours. Her first accommodation was a room in the house of a Mrs Davis in Commercial Street, Senghenydd, who seems to have had a passion for photographs of tombstones on the walls, added to which she preferred candlelight and kept the curtains closed. She would often become angry with her new lodger who spoke no English, causing such fear in my mother that she would hide in her room. '*Che allegria!*' Ten days after her arrival, that same landlady, Mrs Hannah Davies, was one of the witnesses of the marriage between my mother and father in the Church of Holy Souls, Abertridwr.

'I wore black,' my mother said. 'It was the only clothes I had.' She laughed. 'Like I was going to a funeral.' She said that she didn't understand anything the priest was saying to her, but simply repeated the vows parrot-fashion. She was tormented by the idea that this made the marriage invalid.

No one had prepared her for the isolation, particularly as my father took advantage of the extra shifts on offer, and often worked a day and night in succession. In Venice there would be a familiar face as soon as she stepped out into the street. She knew her way around, and had only encountered cars and buses at Piazzale Roma, where they disgorged their passengers before roaring back across the bridge. As a consequence, in Senghenydd she had several near misses as she looked the wrong way crossing the road. She dreaded going to get provisions and having to point and hope she could make herself understood. Some shop keepers were patient, she recalled, while others were not – perhaps some were still suspicious of Italians, who had been released from internment only six years before. She may have been used to going up and over the many bridges of Venice, but they hadn't prepared her legs for the steep streets of the Valleys. She recalled that her calves ached for days before she became used to the enforced exercise.

She came to realise how difficult and strenuous mining was for my father, and she drew her fingers down her cheeks when recalling how gaunt he had become. She was an extremely clean person and tried to keep the household pristine, but the dirt in those early days seemed ever-present. Even the rainwater, she said, seemed black with coal as it scurried down the roadside gutters. She was someone easily provoked into dour memories. Once, the sight of a tin bath outside a shop, now being sold as a chic garden planter, prompted her to recall aloud the daily chore of filling one with hot water in front of the hearth and washing my father. The water would immediately be turned black. The tub was too heavy to empty, so it was necessary to take jugs of the dirty water into the back yard, and then she had to wash his clothes ready for the next shift.

The women of the Valleys were hard-working, and she noted that they didn't preen themselves like Italian women. Welsh women, it seemed to her, only dressed up on Sundays, and even then with modesty and ecclesiastical respect. When I accompanied her to mass back in Italy in her retirement years, her tongue would often click in objection to the abundance of fur coats and jewellery on display.

During those first months in Wales she grew to be enchanted by the houses.

'I was nosy,' she confessed, and throughout that first winter she could not help peering into the front parlours.

She would gaze at families in the glow of firelight; a home and family life that she craved. The well-kept gardens were a novelty, and one day she spotted a man pushing what seemed like a trolley around his front garden. She stopped to watch this strange ritual, curious to see its purpose. He was cutting the lawn, and shooed her away. She hurried on, unable to explain that lawns were the preserve of the Venetian aristocracy.

She got used to the food, eventually, and the local provisions, but she would have to wait another decade or two for Italian produce to become readily available. She was from a country whose cuisine was to become one of the most popular in the world, and yet when she stayed with me on her visits from Italy after she had moved back, she craved nothing more than fish and chips or steak and kidney pie.

On rare days off she and my father got to know the surrounding countryside and she began to appreciate the landscape, which contrasted so much with that of Venice, even the open plains of the Veneto. In later life she would rhapsodise about the dark, dramatic hills and soft colours of Wales. 'So green!' she'd say. She felt that Welsh hills and mountains were approachable; they could be touched, unlike the intimidating and inaccessible-seeming Dolomites of northern Italy.

She and my father would find company and their native tongue in the local Bracchi – one of the many Italian cafés of south Wales. She was given comfort by other Italian women who had joined their husbands and shared her anxieties in those early weeks and months. It was in such a café that someone spoke of the Senghenydd mining disaster, and although it had occurred back in 1913, it played on her mind, especially as she was now with child. Barbara was born exactly a year after my mother's arrival in Wales. By now my mother finally felt settled, and was working as a machinist at the Steinberg clothing factory in Hawthorn.

It was not a mining accident that would threaten Giovanni's life and their future. He developed a persistent cough, but as a smoker this was dismissed, together with his ashen appearance that was surely to do with a lack of sunshine. After mining for less than three years he contracted tuberculosis, and was admitted to the sanatorium in Talgarth. My mother was offered the chance to work there as a domestic, so that she could remain with him and help with his recuperation. She lived in and cleaned the nurses' quarters. She was in awe of their dedication and efficiency, and they supported her when Giovanni's condition worsened to the point that a priest was summoned to administer the last rites.

'*What was I to do?*' she whispered in the interview, her voice echoing a time when she faced returning to Italy a widow and a single parent at twenty-five.

My father underwent an operation to remove half of one lung that was critically infected. My mother then had no choice but to return to Italy in order to leave her daughter with her parents and travel back to Wales to continue to help with my father's two-year long recuperation. She would receive letters from her mother, including one poignant picture of her daughter holding a photograph of her father.

A return to the mines was clearly out of the question. My father needed a new profession or he would risk repatriation to Italy. While in the hospital he took photographs of the other patients, and then had the idea of making Christmas calendars.

'*We sold so many!*'

It was the beginning of a profession that would see him work for BBC Wales and Harlech Television, and be awarded the AMPA (Associate of the Master Photographers Association).

The church of Santa Maria della Salute was built in celebration of the end of the plague. It's a familiar church that's seen on many a postcard of Venice, particularly in its aspect from the Academia bridge. My mother said she had wanted to light a candle in the church to give thanks for my father's recovery. When he was well enough, they returned to Venice to collect their daughter. Her tears of joy at seeing her child after a two-year absence turned to alarm when her daughter hid behind her grandparents, in fear of the 'strangers' who, she was told, were her parents. My mother's tears would readily return in retelling that moment when she feared she had lost her daughter. In time the relationship was slowly rebuilt, though my sister has recollections of confusion on returning to Wales, and perhaps her future difficulties with my father stemmed from that displacement.

My mother had grown deeply fond of Wales, but in the late 1980s my father felt they should retire back to Italy. It seemed the natural thing to do. Neither of them wanted to return to Venice, as they had grown to love the countryside, and so they settled in the gentle hills of the Montello in the Veneto region. My mother was uncertain about the idea, and, in fact, within a few years the decision was reversed. The return to Italy had started well, but after a few months my father began to quarrel with the neighbours. They gave him the nickname '*L'inglese*' (the Englishman). Perhaps he was too sensitive, but he considered himself first an Italian, and then, if anything, a Welshman before an Englishman.

My mother's spoken English retained a Welsh lilt. She often added 'you see,' at the end of her sentences, and, now and again, she exclaimed a long, drawn-out 'Weeell!' As a widow she would cut her lawn, tend to her garden and feed the birds, but there came a time when she grew too lonely.

'*I felt I had no choice,*' she said, but to return to Italy and at least be near her grandchildren.

However, for a few weeks each year she needed to reconnect

with her other homeland, and so she'd stay with me in London and visit friends. She was always aghast at changes she saw in Wales, and particularly in Cardiff, perhaps because she never saw change in her native city – 'Venice is always the same.'

After speaking her native tongue throughout the interview for the Exhibition of Italian Memories in Wales, my mother switched to English for her last words.

'When you leave your own country it's very hard, and you die of nostalgic [sic]... You wish to go back and when the years go by, like this one – fifty years – everything has changed. So you're not very keen to go back, you understand? So obviously after fifty years... you are used to it, this country (Wales). So you can say I love it more to mine.'

My father's ashes were scattered in the Venetian lagoon, according to his wishes. My mother's ashes were placed in her family's vault in the cemetery of Venice (the island of San Michele). The pandemic kept my brother and I away, so it was left to my sister to take my mother's urn across the Ponte della Liberta for the final time, sixty-nine years, almost to the day, after she had left Venice for Wales in 1951.

SIÂN MELANGELL DAFYDD

Son of a Yew Tree

Spring of 2018 was reluctant on the outskirts of the forest of Fontainebleau.

A house, once painted by Sisley, stood a little as though leaning forward towards the *péniches* of the Seine and Loing rivers. It seemed to be held together by the wood of old roses and twists of honeysuckle. My brother, an architect in Wales, once surveyed it and declared he wasn't sure how it held together at all, but I was reassured by the fact that it did, and had done since at least the late 1800s. There were no leaves on my roses and honeysuckle, nor flowers. At the back of the house was a small forest that wasn't yet finding its sap, a place named the Forest of the Violent, although none of the neighbours seemed to recall such a name being used. What sort of violence had happened here? We don't know. We know of the grape vines in the long, long gardens, to grow in summer, harvest in early autumn and store in the cool basements for the Parisians, upstream, at Christmas. We know of the tiny *bouvette* run by Madame del Pippo for the river men, and of the cherry tree she planted outside her kitchen window. Pink in spring, blood red all summer, against the peach walls of the houses on the other side of the Loing. No violence, *non, non,* nobody knew of any violence in those woods.

In that house in spring 2018, a baby was struggling to regain his birth weight. He had been called Ewen, child of the yew tree. And because birth makes nonsense of regular hours, proper behaviour and everyday needs, we spent all day and all night in the living room, sleeping in spurts like cats, window wide open to the forest, to the slabs of sunshine in the afternoons and the whining of trains at night. There we waited for spring and worked on gaining weight. A message arrived from a friend in Cape Cod, Massachusetts:

'I just bought a yew to plant in baby Ewen's honour. The description reads "this yew is a slow growing, soft needled, evergreen shrub". Slow growing, see. Not to worry. '

***

I was named 'Melangell' after the saint's name and the village of Pennant Melangell where my great-grandmother's family came from, just across the Berwyn mountains from where I was raised. My grandfather, who knew what meditation was without knowing its name, spent hours, after he'd retired from farming, walking the Berwyns with no particular aim other than to be with the heather. Once, in his nineties, he followed the trail of a lamb down a steep bank, near Pont Cwm Pydew, searching for the missing creature. Failing to find her, he took a path he knew to be treacherous for himself. Once at the bottom, near the river, he realised that he no longer had the strength to walk back up the muddy slope. The way he saw it, he had two options: die right there or let the river take him somewhere else for better options. He chanced the river, sat in the water, and inched forwards to let the current fill his clothes and take him. He knew this land, the turns of the river and where it might be too turbulent. Also, he knew where the next farm was, and although it was by no means on the very banks of the river, he would try his chances. Somehow, despite the cold water, he managed to pull himself to the riverside and muddy ground when he approached the bottom of that farm garden. There, he hollered and waited – a 90-year-old man sitting in a river, sopping wet, unable to gather the strength to pull himself and the water-weight out. Eventually, confused by a human voice in the reeds, the farmwife found him there, green stable cap still on his head, woollens sopping, and called his family with the news of her discovery. My aunt brought him home. For the first time in memory, he took a bath. The tub was usually a place to store deliveries and tools. In his world bathrooms were places to catch cold; nakedness only led to weakness in his opinion. But the bath, afterwards, she said, was clean.

He couldn't forgo the mountain, even after it had almost defeated him. To sever that connection would have been far more fatal than a bath. So he went in his Land Rover and sat at Derfyn Ddwy Sir, a mountain road that marks the border between two counties, again just to keep the heather in him. He knew exactly where a rare, pure white patch grew. Not lavender-white but quartz-white, eye-white, brittle, shocking on the purple mountain in September. Only he knew. And when the whole Berwyn range blushed to a raging full-bloom colour, miles of purple that glow when seen from a distance, he was sitting in the middle of it. He had seen it coming. He saw, too, the grouse rise as though from nowhere, the odd fox and the soft backs of some grazing sheep. *Grug,* the Welsh word for heather, seems to hold its rugged, insistent nature much better than its English name. Alongside the heather was the yellow of gorse, and a little later in the season came the bright red of rowan berries. Their colours are fiercer this year than ever, but maybe I think that every year. We're approaching that time of the season when my grandmother used to say that a witch would spit on the blackberries and make them 'bad' from then on. The rowans are scooping the ground with laden branches this year. We are made to stop and acknowledge this shocking red. Our blood responds to it with heat and readiness for winter. Are we ready? Rarely. It will be cold, colder than ever. But this is the earth's last blasting message, that we have what it takes to reach spring.

I am in the car, taking a trip I've taken more times than I can remember. Ewen is with me, silent, watching the mountains. We think of travel as going places. It is also leaving places and coming home. Ever since I could drive, I would escape here, over the first cattlegrid in Wales, photographed by Geoff Charles in 1952, my grandfather standing on the left of it, looking wind-dented and embarrassed in a coat he must have inherited from a bigger man. Driving on, we pass Derfyn Ddwy Sir, and then continue over the Berwyns to my great-grandmother's village: Pennant Melangell, on the other side. On the way, I tell my son the story he already knows well.

The naturalist and traveller, Thomas Pennant, related the story of Melangell in the eighteenth century. In various renditions of the story, Melangell is a rebel daughter who escapes her father in Ireland to avoid a forced marriage; she is a pious woman at the centre of an order of nuns in the place now named after her; she is a defiant protector of animals, particularly the hare – lambs of Melangell, according to Pennant – in the face of masculine forces of hunting, represented by Prince Brochwel. The year was 604 AD. She saved the hare from him by giving it shelter under her dress. She can be virgin, beauty, activist, pacifist, nun, asylum seeker or hermit, depending how you tell the story. Her tale was told for over eight hundred years, passed down from generation to generation before it was first written down in the late fifteenth century in the *Historia Divae Monacellae* (the Latin name for Melangell). When Pennant visited the valley in the late eighteenth century, he found that the story was being recounted, not read. This was unsurprising, given that most of the valley's inhabitants wouldn't have been able to read, let alone understand Latin. Pennant wrote the story, but as good storytellers do – and as the locals had no doubt done themselves – he also added his own touches. In Pennant's version, when Prince Brochwel raises his horn to his mouth, ready to urge on the hounds in the hunt, having already discovered the hare under Melangell's hem, no sound comes out, and instead it sticks to his lips. Pennant gives pause to Brochwel's crime with that punishment. But ultimately, this woman, Melangell, had powers that made her skirt an impenetrable barrier even when Brochwel tried a second time.

While Melangell has many identities, she is now officially the Patron Saint of Animals, buried here in the middle of grouse-shooting terrain. I look for the hare whenever I visit – the Celtic animal, who, since my travels to India, has become somehow akin to the goddess Lakshmi as a symbol of prosperity, good fortune and abundance. But I have only seen stone, ink and oak hares in Pennant Melangell, all these years.

I take the twenty-minute drive with Ewen in the back. I slow down to a safe speed to avoid killing the hundreds of pheasants as soon as we are past Llangynnog. We head to the church, where we will spend slower time still in the graveyard, among the yews, scanning the mountains. No hares.

Pennant – *pen y nant* – meaning 'head of the stream' is not an uncommon name in Wales. Here it must refer to nant Ewyn, which has enough *ewyn* – froth – and fierceness in most seasons to create electricity for the cottage neighbouring the church. The church is surrounded by the mountains that I've just crossed. Up ahead is a Mohawk of forestry trees, abruptly felled in a straight line. The carpark in Pennant Melangell is almost always quiet. The pineapple weed, pollinated by car tyres, doesn't look dusty and flattened here, but worth picking for tea. I pull in and, as always, hope that we are alone, that we will have the place to ourselves. Today the carpark only has three ducks. Ewen declares them too ugly to be ducks. I show him their feet. Later, I learn that they are Muscovy. They are strange, red wart-faced creatures. We hear geese getting all bothered in the field above.

Once through the lychgate, there is a female yew tree to my right. In September and October, like so many plants in our climate in that season, the female yew gives fruit. There, on the ground, I see one red berry; it's oddly perfect, a shop-bought bead shape, as though someone's necklace had broken right here in the yarrow.

The flesh of this yew berry, the aril, is the only part of the tree that isn't poisonous. Even the seed in its centre is poisonous, as well as the bark, the wood, the soft needles. I stop there and point. I tell Ewen not to touch. We have gathered blackberries and raspberries, haw and sloe, rowan and elderberry. 'This beautiful one right here, we never, ever eat this,' I say. I lift him to my hip so that his eyes are level with the lower branches. We point but don't touch. I think of the woman I once knew who said that she and her friends used to eat them on the way to school and spit out the seed. But she was someone I learned not always to believe. I often wonder about that story and those children. How did they know to spit? Who dared first, and how did their expressions change on tasting it? Ewen is curious enough to crush one with his knee as soon as he's on the ground again. He says it's sticky, which it is; despite its redness, it seeps a translucent, glue-like substance. But this three-year-old can describe the pixie ears on a leaf of common sorrel to his grandmother and he knows I'm serious when it comes to what *not* to eat and what we leave for the birds.

Four ancient yews stand here in an almost circular churchyard. Yews grow in places which were considered sacred before they were Christian. In this case, the church lies within a Bronze Age site. The yews are considered to be almost two thousand years old. But I feel as though I'm hearing a child repeating their favourite joke every time someone makes a claim about the age of a yew. These trees are tricksters. The heartwood of the tree rots from the inside, taking with it any rings that might help date it, or the possibility of carbon dating. And so, many a town will claim their yew to be the oldest. We are left to date them by their surroundings, such as timber in ancient buildings, and by stories.

The path leads to the church, of course, but we veer off. Not left, to the yew always bejewelled with visitors' gemstones, feathers, ribbons, prayers. We know our path. We know that to the west of the church is a yew that can hold a person's body until they are almost all lost in the tree. You just step right into a hip-width chimney and look upwards to the tree's canopy. Place your belly to the tree. There the bark is in the shape of a standing wolf-man, some say, and you'll be enveloped together. I am never at ease, even when I stand back and search for him in the bark patterns. This popular yew isn't the one which usually holds our attention.

We circle the church, past the rounded apsidal sanctuary. During the restoration of the church in the 1980s, a radical decision was made to demolish this part of the church altogether and to rebuild the east end as a semi-circular apse, on the footings of an apse that was much, much older still. In 1988, the bones of a woman from about the time of Melangell were discovered beneath a large stone in the floor of a small, semi-circular room, at this eastern end of the church. Early Christian churches used this semi-circular space in their layout, so the room could have been built on an original, much older feature. The place where the bones lay was known as the Cell y Bedd, or 'grave cell'; when the bones were discovered, they were transferred to the rebuilt shrine. We walk around the outside curve and beyond where Melangell lies, to a male yew, apparently huge even in 1848 when it featured in a sketch of the church by R. Kyrke Penson.

By 2000, a diary written by botanist Fergus Kinmonth as he collected material for the millennium yew project described a 'male tree measuring 31' 9" [in girth] with a massively spreading root mass that tapers to a waist then flares again to support four enormous limbs'. There are also remnants of two seemingly dead branches, although there is a small amount of new growth on one – dead is never dead on a yew tree. They are not considered trees of longevity for nothing.

They say that in 1987, the ground beneath one of these Melangell yews was covered with industrial salt to mimic snow for a film commemorating the life of Ann Griffiths, the nineteenth century Welsh hymn writer. The salt was left where it was, to wash into the soil and eventually reach the roots. It was thought the yew wouldn't survive; even the foliage showed signs of damage. The tree of longevity, killed by industrial salts? But in 1998 the Ancient Yew Group reported that they couldn't even detect any sign of harm! If the church here lies within a Bronze Age site, it has been considered a place of sanctuary long before memory and has suffered more than salt. Only the trees know the full story.

***

I named my son after these trees in Pennant Melangell. He was born in a place that was bookended with violence, a place I didn't even know I needed to escape at that time, so I named him after a safe place. Before his birth, so I made many lists: things for a hospital bag, baby necessities in order of age by three-month periods, foods to stockpile and freeze, phone numbers, the names of women who supported me. I made the preparations and purchases alone and was ridiculed for my care. I somehow convinced myself that those who showed the baby love were nourishing his or her growth, that any hatred would simply not penetrate. A frightened body has tight muscles and shallow breath. And that is how, for a little more time, I kept the baby safe, as though tucked under my skirt. An abused woman's body knows she is unsafe, even if her mind resists.

A month or so before his birth, I sat in the kitchen. February,

Formica yellow table, a notebook open on an empty page, and I decided on that day that it would be our project to visit yew trees together. Just like that. It seems utterly ridiculous now, this idea, as though an inquiry of some sort would serve us, or even save us. What might actually have saved us was to leave right there and then, but I looked out at the Loing and continued my nest-making. My scrawled 'visit yews' appeared on a list in the back of a Moleskine, along with other books and articles in process, some barely begun, but it was maybe the tiny beginning of something that would eventually shed light on what is poisonous and what is not.

From my seat, I would look up from time to time. Above the doorway, a postcard-sized painting of Y Santes Melangell on wood, two pothos plants dangling low. Outside, there were fewer *péniches* around at that time, and I could look out right onto the water. I recognised the silhouette of a kingfisher standing on a reed, smaller always than I expect. It was still and I was still. I had only ever seen them in flight, always fleeting. And there we were, together, perched. It went for a fish, eventually. And I, heavily pregnant, silently placed my hopes of a heathy and safe life for my child on the tree of longevity.

Ewen announces that he's an unkind ghost living in the yew. He has designated a bedroom at the base of one branch, a place to have tea in another. The base of each of the three huge branches, starting from the main platform, creates a bowl – enough space for two small people to occupy. I am allowed to have tea in one, and he serves me an elder leaf.

All around are the colours of the bark: ochres, crimsons and aubergines in flakes. He gestures in whatever way he feels a ghost would. Above him there are tufts of young twigs, upward-growing beards on older branches. One branch – typically for a yew – once bent too low, I suspect, and was cut off. Other branches seem rotten, but I know well enough that this is the yew's way.

And of this unkind ghost: one day, a stone tells him to be kind, he says, and he changes and becomes kind, *caredig.*

'Don't be afraid of this tree, Mam,' he says, in Welsh.

Frothing about his feet are the tapering leaves of an elder. No berries. It seems to grow into the yew. I step away and listen to his story of the ghost's life in the various compartments of the yew. The ghost is *caredig* and can climb huge things, *caredig* and makes wind in the trees, *caredig* and then I hear a mumble which may also include some English. From there, I can take a photograph of him being wind, being spirit. His arms are conjuring charms. The photograph captures something else that the eye can't see: an orb, giant, eye-like, appears around him once I click. He is caught in a gesture of a magician, palms towards the inner tree. The orb, I think, allows him safety, the upper curve a full rainbow.

As is our habit these days, I share this photograph online. Ewen's face is towards the yew. We only see the back of his hair like a patch of yellow Stag's Horn fungus, and this orb, framing him in place in the yew. I know that many will believe that the spirit world is responsible for the presence of light matter in dark places like this, especially in the cradle of a yew tree in a graveyard. I also know about backscatter: the way light captures particles in the air that are near invisible to the naked eye. I believe both, today.

Later someone leaves a comment, on seeing the photograph, that in the presence of the yew, but also the elder, is a force protecting this child. I need to believe my online friend. I need this photograph, just as I need our safety to always, always be confirmed, repeated, reminded. It has been my mantra. I came here to whisper my worries to an old tree but found that I played house and pretended to be a ghost instead. Better. We are safe. We are safe. This is more powerful when confirmed by a yew and by others who see clearly.

MARY-ANN CONSTANTINE

King Stevan's Roads

Donnet e rei un amzer e grouézou en henteu a vorh de vorh hag en dud e griou forh.

A time will come when the roads will criss-cross from village to village and the people will cry out in despair.

– Eighteenth-century Breton prophecy,
    attributed to Ar Roué Stevan

Brittany. Breiz-Izel. At the turn of its twenty-first century I was deep into its nineteenth, a world of people walking. Charcoal burners and rag-collectors, sardine-packers, itinerant tailors, pilgrims. And with them or after them on the green roads, the muddy lanes, came collectors of tradition, tracking ballads of shipwreck and murder, stories of saints, of the restless dead.

Many of their journeys were loops, annual and cyclical. For both the dead and the living, I suppose, there were places you needed to be at fixed points in time. My own visits had no such regularity, not even the regularity of a carefully planned and well organised research trip. For a period of three or four years I would get myself over there and, with decent French and inadequate Breton, gather material haphazardly from people who really knew about the place and its past, who were glad I was interested, and were generous enough to share. Looking back at those journeys now, and at much later revisitings in very different times, I can see some patterns. They are mostly to do with roads.

We stayed for a while on a small island outside Morlaix, at Saint-Martin-des-Champs. It's an island of good sense and good humour, of strawberries and shallots, farmed in plots around the house. The requisite apple tree was in bloom when we arrived. The house, nineteenth-century, rather fine, is down a curving gravelled drive framed by suitable plants: azalea, rhododendron, sky-blue hydrangea. The shrubs of the bourgeoisie. There is something of them, too, in the delicate metal wreck of a burnt-out glasshouse poised against one wall. But they are workers here now, and the living is got from the strawberries and shallots, a part-time job on the local paper, and the guests, who stop here because it seems convenient, discover smooth white sheets in carved wooden beds, and parquet floors so polished their little dogs slip around with splayed legs, and a feast of a breakfast next morning. If they're the kind of guests who listen, the humour will be thrown in *gratis*.

You can't see it from inside. The trees around the island are fairly tall and thick enough to hide how close it is; the low growl, behind glass, is deadened too. Arriving in the normal course of things, by car, you will have taken it for granted. But we were marooned there and soon learned what the children of the house will learn when their legs are long enough to take them looking for the edges of their island: you can't get off on foot. It sits in a noose formed by the *voie-express* and a tangle of slip roads, with a current of cars and lorries too strong and unpredictable to risk. No footbridge or tunnel or lights or holy staff of God to cut through the flow.

You *can* do it on foot. We did, many times. To get to the bus stop, or the bright lights of the giant supermarket, even for a loaf of bread, you set off crabwise and approach laboriously, following the knot under and over as though you were a car. A revelation: the loops they do in seconds take chunks out of pedestrian hours – ten minutes, five minutes, five again. There are no pavements, just verges of dirt or grass, some of them bravely planted with flowers, sloping up from the road to the fences of the various warehouses of the *zone artisanale*. These have energetic, irritating names and sell cheap shoes and factory-price clothes to those who have cars to come for them. Walking past a garage maddens three dogs, who fling themselves – every time – at the metal fence. Without wheels, you are a provocation, obliged to chance yourself across the neck of a slip road that feeds the *voie-express*. You are a menace. We flinch at every hoot of the horn.

We learned to reckon with the road in different weathers. In the sun you get tired and dusty, traipsing along the verge like something from Steinbeck. But the rain is worse, the heavy blinding rain, when you can hear them coming and they cannot see you, and every one that goes past is a slap in the face. I think now, looking back, that it was a day like that. We were heading back to the house, it was raining, the traffic lashed past, and we came to the third roundabout, where the turn-off to the left is the beginning of the long final straight, past the warehouses and the furious dogs, to the island. From the far side of this roundabout we heard a horrible sound, the whimpering of an animal in pain, probably a dog – a noise to make you afraid and sick with pity. I suppose the road had taken away all our courage, because it is only now it occurs to me that we could have done anything other than what we did: say nothing, hold hands very tightly and push on through the rain towards the house.

Roads are different when you're the driver, of course. We acquired a car; we acquired a baby. My research headed off after a new group of songs, and we came back for some geographical context. This time it rained potatoes. We rolled off the ferry at Roscoff into the dark, July rain lashing at the windows. And soon, where there should have been Leon with its big fields and bigger sky, there was more darkness, with just the road coming at us bathed in orange light, its markings and signposts shining bright and self-sufficient. We drive in a British convoy inside the glow of the wide ribbon of road, gradually entranced by the lights and the rain, the names of places, resisting the appeals in English to eat, sleep, buy huge quantities of alcohol. We pass the solid granite corners of old houses, the promises of supermarkets to come. The lines on the road are hypnotic. The baby is asleep in the back; neither of us needs to speak.

And then, along the borders of the road, we start to notice dark patches of potatoes. They get thicker, the road cuts through them, pushing them aside, behind the white lines. We speed gently through dark masses of knobbly potatoes, and the hard rain gets harder. The piles grow, spill over, the potatoes seem likely to encroach; and then there are yellow street-sweeping vehicles and a plastic ribbon across the road. A *flic* points us off into the night, into the streets of St Pol where the flow of British cars divides and dissipates like water in a marsh, down a handful of little channels, none of them the obvious way through.

Of course the authorities have dealt with worse, with cauliflowers even, Breton farmers often being angry and inclined to throw things. But in the sleepy hypnosis of the road trip it felt like the aftermath of a natural disaster: all those brave men-in-uniform, with their lorries and emergency plastic ribbons, and the rain pouring off our windscreens under the orange lights, in the wake of one of the worst potato-storms within living memory. A snippet of a Vannetais song from the early 1900s now reads like a weird premonition:

Kaer en doè er sorsourez troein ha distroein hi hartow
Dond e hrèi en owlow doar tré bidèg er muriow.

All in vain were the wise-woman's spells
The potatoes came on steady, right up to the walls.

We go round St Pol twice and find a way back onto the glowing road, where the potatoes continue sporadically and then gradually disappear. Eventually we meet the slip road for our island and glide in swiftly, easily, to our waiting welcome.

Roads found their way into my research through a poem about an old woman who built them: Ahès the witch, a queen, a crone, a metaphor – who knows – for the power and reach of the Roman legions. She is associated with Carhaix (Karaez), a hub for Roman roads, and has parallels with other road-building queens, like Elen Lluydauc from the Welsh tale of *Macsen Wledig*. In the nineteenth century much ink was spilled trying to prove how, where, when, her legend appeared: I followed some of it into a scholarly spaghetti junction, and emerged not much the wiser. The poem may well have been pastiche, a bit of antiquarian wishful thinking, but I learned that roads crowd other kinds of Breton popular tradition, and loom large in the apocalyptic prophecies of itinerant preachers such as Ar Roué Stevan (King Stevan), a ragged vagabond bearer of esoteric information, who foresaw, with horror, a time when Brittany would be so criss-crossed with roads that the people would cry out in despair.

I also learned that the great late-twentieth-century collectors and ethnographers I tagged along with tend to do their collecting in cars. So I never really had the time or will-power to properly follow the earlier ones on foot, nor their informants, nor the poor doomed people in their tragic songs, who sometimes walk until their feet bleed. (Back then – and this is true – you could hire a pilgrim to do the miles for you between the stone chapels and the holy wells: in God's eyes, apparently, outsourced suffering still counts). As a result, the parts of Brittany I know are all broken up and scattered, and some memories have no clear location.

A very old woman is said to know a version of a nineteenth-century song I'm working on, and I am taken to see her. She is in bed in a back room in a small dark cottage, no longer able to sing, rocking back and forth, and I'm frightened at the sight of what should be normal: a grandmother, a great aunt, looked after at home, disintegrating. I'm not used to this, but my companion is; he moves between languages and chats at ease with the family. I think he recorded her ten years earlier, and nothing that disturbs me here is unusual to him. We stay a little while, get back in the car, move on.

There are fixed points, of course. The research centre is on the top floor of a building that looks a bit like a ship, with windows facing out over the grey port city of Brest to the sea.

An efficient research student would have taken lodgings near the library. A brave one would have found a place in the country with a Breton-speaking family. Brest was too vast, too grey, too incomprehensibly sprawling for me, and I could not get to know it by walking. I did know, as one might technically know something learned at school, that the city had been flattened during the war, when the Allies and the Germans destroyed virtually everything in their attempts to control this most strategic of westerly ports. And when people cheerily (and often) said, in the rainy streets *il pleut sans cesse sur Brest* I knew they were quoting; I think I even knew Jacques Prévert's poem, probably as a *chanson*. What I don't understand is why it is only now, as I sit and try to pull bits of Brittany onto the page, that the knowledge of that complete erasure (*Brest, dont il ne reste plus rien*) changes its quality, its heft, becomes something dreadful and full of meaning. I find now that Brest features in articles by geographers who use the term 'place annihilation'. And I remember the ethnographer telling me how he watched the bombardment as a little boy from his grandparents' house, and was enthralled.

Instead, I chose Morlaix/Montroulez, a small, pretty estuary town whose river marks the line where Tregor and Leon meet, with a marina and a *vieux quartier*, all cobbled streets and half-timbered houses, and gardens hanging over stone walls. It is beloved of English tourists, especially those with yachts. There are churches, museums, a library where I could work, and many cafés; best of all is the viaduct, striding in beautiful arches across the town. It reminded me of Durham, where I grew up. The most Parisian of the cafés, the Grand Café de la Terrasse, with its interior of big mirrors and a fine curving staircase, spills its tables onto the square close to one of the viaduct's supports. Coming on foot from the direction of St Martin you can make your way to it through steep narrow streets down scores of little steps. Of course I brought my mother here when she came to visit.

At the top of the hill, close against the top of the viaduct where the railway it carries heads for Brest, or back to Rennes, there is a plaque near a stone chapel. I passed it quite often and had doubtless read it the first time I saw it. It stopped my mother properly, though, because the date it marks, 29 January 1943, is the day she was born, and the lives commemorated are those of thirty-nine primary school children, aged between four and seven, and their teacher, who died, along with twenty-seven other civilians not named here, when the British Allied Forces bombed the viaduct from the air. The aim was to break the supply chain to Brest, yet there were other viaducts on this line in areas far less densely populated, and the line was operational again after only eight days. The Vichy government must have hoped the strike would turn all of Morlaix against the Allies; but in December 1943, eleven months later, an attack on German forces in the town resulted in the round-up and arrest of sixty men, who were subsequently deported to Buchenwald. The pretty square with the fine café is now renamed the Place des Otages.

The legacy of a shockingly botched British mission sits uncomfortably alongside a Resistance-focused memorialisation of the war, and subsequent attempts to commemorate the loss, as a recent historian has shown, have been caught in a tangle of competing ideologies. Much of the iconography associated with the 1954 memorial chapel, Notre Dame des Anges, evokes the 'sacrifice' of little angels taken in their purity straight to Paradise; they rise as a flock of doves. A Breton lament or *gwerz* composed in the traditional style to raise money for its construction refers obliquely to the 'cruel sparrowhawk' who destroys them. That hawk casts another kind of shadow: the alignment (sometimes real, but also imagined or assumed) of the Breton-language cultural revival with the occupying German forces. I was at least notionally aware of some of this, but still my younger self disappoints me: escaping from unsettling Brest to reassuring Morlaix, and reading nineteenth-century texts through scholarship shaped by the twentieth, she could have made more effort to understand the connections between them. The war lies like a film of oil across Breton history: sometimes it is transparent and you forget it's there, but you are always looking through it.

Twenty years later, there were invitations to come back. I did, once or twice, for conferences. Not long ago I found myself in a place that mimicked, but like a terrible dream, the geospatial set up of our first Morlaix guest house. This was a motel, a proper Hitchcock *Psycho* motel, once again islanded by dual carriageway and slip roads and warehouses in the bleakest outer orbit of a beautiful city whose *centre ville* is all paved open squares and plane-trees, looped with rivers, crossed by stone bridges. I was dropped off here by a courteous conference organiser, who had come to meet my late train and driven out of his way to see me safely lodged. It was December, raining and bitterly cold. It took us twenty minutes to open the door, a complex process involving a combination safe box, a card, and several phone calls to automated systems to receive magical activating numbers that didn't activate anything. No people. The room I finally got into was a little dark box facing a forecourt on the ground floor. There were noises I couldn't understand. Three nights, I'd been booked for. I forgot to feel hungry. I got under the bedclothes and planned an escape. Again, entirely without human contact – and yes, I'm so old that this still seems to me to be utterly strange – I found my phone and booked myself a bright, first floor self-catering flat in the heart of the lovely city, and then I slept. In the morning I discovered the section of the motel that had been locked the night before, and found a girl there, standing at a desk, next to a machine that dispensed fruit, pots of flavoured yoghurt and plastic-wrapped croissants. I said there had been a mistake and asked how to get into town on foot. She had no idea, but did her best to explain how one might.

I think now how baffled they must be, the ghosts of all those pilgrims and labourers, vagabonds and prophets, who once carried information along road networks that made more sense; I think of them pooling in anxious invisible groups, in areas from which they cannot easily escape. But I did escape, and it took me back to those days of slogging along the verges of the *voie-express*. This time, ridiculously, I was dragging a little wheeled suitcase and knew but did not care how odd I must look to the cars zipping by. I finally came bowling down a sloping concrete underpass into a tangle of roundabouts and shops that could have been anywhere in the northern hemisphere, and found myself facing a puzzling set of bus stops. Here I spent some time with the phone held aloft, turning round and round trying to work out where town might be, and then a bus pulled up behind me and I got on to ask the driver which route I needed. This one, he said. I had no idea how to pay, not having had a chance to get money. *Madame*, he said, *le dimanche c'est gratuit*. The half-hour drive to the beautiful city was one long sigh of relief.

Four years earlier, in 2015, a similar conference had taken place in the beautiful late-medieval manor house of Kernault, near Mellac in Cornouailles/Kerne. The building is of honey-coloured stone, with clean, simple lines, a big hall, grassy courtyard and grounds. I found several old friends there, including the ethnologist and his wife, both frailer now, but in different ways. It was difficult to believe that his innate and appealing impracticality could have worsened, but it had – more difficult to see her sharp mind ragged with disconnections, her face suddenly troubled or bright and full of wonder. Accommodation for delegates was once again in an identikit Ibis Motel (less sinister, bright and plastic, but equally noosed by huge fast roads). I was tired and on edge when I arrived. Mid-November, like December, is no time to travel: the dark crushes in around you too quickly, and anxieties about not being able to get away on foot rose up and swamped me. I was rescued by two friends and pulled into the warmth of a lovely cottage belonging to one of them in a nearby village. I would be even more glad of this kindness later.

The final day was a Friday and the conference ended with a dinner. I was placed next to the great-grandson of the subject of my paper – a viscount who, early in the nineteenth century, had collected and published Breton songs and had travelled to an eisteddfod in south Wales; like us, he was wined and dined by interesting people, and his letters home are vivid, gossipy slices of their lives. He was in his early twenties at the time, so, in the weird collapsible way of time and history, the great-grandson is nearly three times the age of the young man in the letters, and I'm old enough to be his mother: we laugh at him a bit, at his tendency to overdramatise and to think he is the centre of everything (although, I suppose, at the conference, he is). Here and now in the big hall the evening progresses and everyone talks; the ethnologist and his wife are close by. She gazes with pleasure at the pattern on my dress and says how beautiful it is, *c'est vraiment réussi*. The talk across the table in multiple directions is a warm connective hum, and we loop and reloop through then and now, exchanging threads of ourselves, our different kinds of knowledge. It gets later and later, and although we must all be bone tired after the long day the talk continues, back and forth. Then I see she is crying. *Les pauvres enfants*, she is saying. *O les pauvres à Paris*. I think that the neural pathways must have twisted abruptly to make her cry like this, tears shining on her cheeks. But no, she has a phone.

My friends come up behind the chair and bend over me and say we're going, come on, something's happened, we're going to go home now, we should find out more. And under the rafters of the big hall little groups are scattering, gently embracing, kissing their farewells and trying to learn more from their friends and relations in Paris. Everyone in Brittany has someone there. And I remember the three of us in the cottage then as the news came in of the bombs at the Stade de France, the shootings in bars and cafés, and the massacre at the Bataclan. The figures kept rising. France shut its borders.

It is harder now, in a world of fluctuating border restrictions, to convey the shock of this at the time. Travel, including my own journey home the following day, appeared impossible. For much of the night we tried to find out more, and in the end simply got up very early and drove to the station. A train came, unexpectedly, exactly as scheduled, and I got on, thinking to get as far as I could towards home, where I very much wanted to be. I remember a quietness in the train, but it was nothing like the dreadful silence coming off the streets between Montparnasse and the Gare du Nord. The Eurostar was running, with heightened security. And eventually trains did get me home, to the west coast of Wales, in a long curve that took me through two capital cities, one in shock, one apprehensive, skirting the peripheries of another kind of hell. In 1946 Prévert saw rainclouds move across the skies above annihilated Brest, like dogs crawling off to die (*des nuages / Qui crèvent comme des chiens [...] qui vont pourrir au loin*). If I had thought about it then as I am thinking about it now I could perhaps have heard them whimpering.

KANDACE SIOBHAN WALKER

Clearances

1 PINE

Below, the landscape is cut into neat parcels of land. We are flying over Georgia in the dry heat of early afternoon. A voice over the comm tells the crew to prepare for landing, and reports the approximate local time. It is July. The airport's white-roofed hangars and fields of grey tarmac appear underneath us, slowly expanding as we descend.

Wheeling my suitcase through the wide, beige-carpeted hallways, I feel overwhelmed by the American airport experience. Stateside, I am a rube. I approach a vending machine for water, only to find that it contains phone chargers and earphones. I feel like I have walked in on a capitalist's dream of the future, where everything is a mall. Western cities are all alike in the same way that shopping centres mirror each other, and airports are their love child: a perfect intersection of futurism and the free market. Walking past the same chain restaurants and cocktail bars as the place I departed from, I feel increasingly aware of the airport's achromatic neutrality. Even the displays of local history have had their particularities smoothed away, so that the black-and-white photographs that accompany stories of triumph and adversity feel simultaneously universal and unrecognisable. Only the view from the window-walls, of the pines beyond the runways, lets me know that I have travelled at all.

But the South in the summertime is a strange animal. It feels like home and unlike home. Because I am a descendant of slaves; because I did not grow up here. It's green and wide open and haunted, like Wales where I was raised, but also arid and flat and conversational, unlike that place. I walk through a covered white and terracotta approximation of a colonial courtyard at the centre of Hilton Head International Airport, past the gift store and an arcade. Outside arrivals, sweating in the taxi bay's superficial concrete shade, I wait for my brother's partner's black truck. Everywhere, the tarmac shimmers.

Escaping the multi-storey carpark, we drive through Pooler, a small city with a population of some 25,000 people – white Americans in the majority. Drive fifteen minutes east of Pooler and you'll arrive in Savannah, the first city in the last colony established by the British on the land that would become America. An engraving made by one Peter Gordon in early spring, 1734, shows a rectangular packet of land that has been cleared away for the building of the 'town of Savannah'. The settlement is surrounded on all sides by 'vast woods of pine-trees' that reach the horizon.

We aren't heading east, though – we're southbound. We drive down a slip road, past buildings that look brand new and outdated. A shopping complex has a red and white mock-lighthouse at the centre of its parking lot. I marvel at the wideness of the roads and the height of the signs –

advertisements for drive-thrus and churches and hotels – that border each street. I'm awed by the sheer scale of the landscape. Everything is strange and gargantuan: the wide, plain-like strip malls and outlets; our jeep overshadowed by queues of monster freight trucks, as tall as a double-decker bus; even the rough young pine trees. Occasionally we pass clusters of grey, emaciated tree trunks, the ground around them ghostly and bare. These burnt-out clearings punctuate the happy, opaque pine forests flanking the highway. I don't know enough about the land to tell whether they are the aftermath of wildfires or controlled burns.

We're heading south on Interstate 95, past fields and streetlights. Pooler is a city with big stretches of lawn and brush between the buildings, so it feels strangely rural. Below the interstate overpass, on Louisville Rd, traffic lights hang against the sky on near-invisible wires. I am comforted by the green, open spaces. Without grazing sheep or cows, the fields have the appearance of wilderness. But I know better. This land is vacant, but not wild. Every pasture we pass was once known, lived on and cared for, then cleared, then colonised and settled – sometimes the other way around, often violently. The fields appear uninhabited now, but the land belongs to someone and it is owned by someone, which is not the same thing. Later, I ask around and get my answer: this is Muskogee Creek land. Past Brunswick, a little ways further south, the land belongs to the Timucua who, according to an encyclopaedia, are no longer here but, according to descendants of the Timucuans, remain.

The roads narrow and bend, and I smell saltwater. Then I know that we are nearing the dock in Meridian, where the day's last ferry will take me to Sapelo.

2 SAPELO

At Marsh Landing, near the mouth of the Duplin River, the Katie Underwood slows and pulls up by the dock. That is the ferry's name, after the midwife who delivered my grandmother Cornelia, and many others on the island. My father picks me up and we drive northeast to my grandmother's house. The welcome sign at the community's edge declares a population of seventy-one, but in reality the figure is less than fifty.

Turning off Airport Road onto the East-West Autobahn, the pine trees clear and a handful of buildings appear ahead of us. We pass by the community library, which is a blue bungalow with a white deck, and the white clapboard Sapelo Island Cultural & Revitalization Society (SICARS) building. The library's windows are dark – the woman who runs it now lives on the mainland and commutes. We park in my grandparents' yard then get out and walk. We pass behind the Graball Country Store, the island's only shop – generally residents buy groceries on the mainland – which is run by my family, past the holiday rental and a trailer on cinder blocks, under a twisted tree decorated with moss.

'You not staying in The Wallow,' says my grandmother – referring to the inn. 'You're staying in the house. We moved the boys in together and made you a room.'

The blue house, the inn and the store sit on about an acre of land. Overgrown fields partially obscure houses in the middle distance – houses owned by neighbours, aunts and uncles, elders and cousins. Like the library, my grandmother's house is built on a small foundation, less than three feet tall. Changes to federal building codes mean the multi-million-dollar holiday homes that have been popping up across the island stand on eight-foot pilings, towering above the homes lived in by the island's full-time residents, who are largely black. Older buildings on Sapelo are easy to recognise: the houses are rain-beaten and low, hidden among the trees and close to the earth.

Hogg Hummock, sometimes spelled Hog Hammock, is the last Saltwater Geechee community in the Sea Islands. The Sea Islands are a long barrier chain stretching from South Carolina, through Georgia and down to Florida. The grassy salt marshes and winding waterways that separate the islands from mainland America, as well as the dense flora that covers many of the islands, offer the south-eastern coast protection from storms rolling in from the sea. South of Sapelo, you will find St Simon's Island, Sea Island, Jekyll Island and Amelia Island. To the north, Ossabaw, Daufuskie and St Helena's, to name a few. Some of the islands are accessible by bridges, but not Sapelo.

At her kitchen table, my grandmother explains that when she was born there were still five communities on Sapelo: Belle Marsh, Racoon Bluff, Lumber Landing, Shell Hammock and Hogg Hummock. She describes her early childhood as 'a paradise', hidden away from the realities of the world. With the exception of the Reynolds Mansion towards the south end of the island – built on the site of the island's former plantation house – the inhabitants of these communities were almost exclusively the descendants of enslaved Africans. That was in 1945, when the island's population was somewhere around three hundred. Now only Hogg Hummock remains.

The cousins want to take me on a tour. We pile onto a golf cart – normally rented out to tourists by our grandfather, Frank – and turn right out of the yard. We pass a sign for LULA'S

KITCHEN. RIB 'N' CHICKEN! LOW COUNTRY BOIL!

Lula's is the only restaurant on the island. The younger cousins point out people's houses. Many have white and red 'for sale' signs driven into the dirt by the porch. The clapboard on a few houses is painted haint blue, so spirits will fly over the roof and not in through the keyhole. There are abandoned vehicles in driveways, in fields. A yellow tractor sits by the side of the road, greenery erupting from its windows like a party dress. I ask who it belongs to and my seven-year-old cousin, who is dangling his bare feet off the side of the golf cart, says: 'It belongs to me!'

As we drive further north, the forest grows darker and indistinct around us. Light sparkles abruptly between the leaves, like sunshine on water. Giant oaks, arching overhead and sweeping towards the ground, make the island's interior feel dense and wild. Southern live oaks are the state tree of Georgia. In every direction, a cartography of tree limbs expands across my view. A traveller in 1940 described the trees' 'ghostly beauty': some of them are hundreds of years old. Older than the island's name, older than this country.

This is what is called a maritime forest, and it once covered most of Sapelo. I take pictures of the grey Spanish moss draped over the branches, admiring the way it makes lace out of the forest canopy. It is neither Spanish nor a moss, but a bromeliad. The story is that the Native Americans called it *itla-okla*, meaning tree hair. But the French used to call it *barbe espagnol*, or Spanish beard. In retaliation, the Spanish started calling it *cabello francés*, but that didn't stick. We pass a small ashen clearing like the scorched groves on the mainland – another controlled burn, as I now know. Pine trees, it's explained to me, are good for industry, but bad for the island's natural ecosystem. Without intervention, wherever the pines encroach on the original forest, the live oaks will not grow back.

Driving past a holiday home, we are suddenly made small. The structure towers over the golf cart and even some of the trees. Its height is discomforting; its whiteness is cold against the leaves; even the supportive pilings are brilliant white. The front door is flanked by neoclassical columns and there's a pretty, naturalistic pattern carved into the decorative frieze. The holiday home looks, I realise, like a plantation house on stilts.

'Who lives there?' I ask.

My little cousin answers, 'Nobody live there, except when it's hot!'

After a second we are returned to the forest. There are no more buildings now, only ruins and trees. Building here is prohibited. Legally, this land belongs to the state.

The oaks surrender to a wide, flat field. We have arrived at Chocolate. It was once a plantation, but there is no sign now of the cotton fields that used to grow here. The ruined slave dwellings we can see are built from tabby, which is sometimes called coastal concrete. Tabby is made using water, sand, seashells and lime. A barn, restored in the 1920s, shows signs of decay – in places, its smooth outer walls have flaked away to reveal the original tabby structure underneath. There was once a big house here too, overlooking the salt marshes. It is gone now, dismantled by the years and weather, or maybe by emancipated slaves who used its materials to build their own homes elsewhere on the island.

Driving home, we pass an almost invisible turning – a dirt road that disappears into the bush – and someone says, 'Down there's Belle Marsh.' Like Shell Hammock and Lumber Landing and Raccoon Bluff, nobody lives at Belle Marsh anymore. Its last black landowner, Hicks Bailey, was my great-grandfather. He was born in the old house at Belle Marsh in 1903. Hicks hadn't wanted to move, but the then-owner of the big house on the south end of the island wanted his property. He was told he could keep his job or he could keep his land. In 1950, he packed up his family and moved down to Hogg Hummock.

***

I wake up late. My grandmother's house is quiet. The cousins are playing in the yard. Outside, the light is so bright and total that I struggle to even look at the sky. My grandfather loans me a golf cart. I drive around, sometimes to the beaches or to the north end or down whichever dirt road catches my eye.

At Nanny Goat Beach one afternoon, a tourist vacationing with her young children tells me that what she loves about Sapelo is its isolation. The tourist wears a wide-brimmed hat and dark, narrow sunglasses. 'Isn't it beautiful?' she asks. But when she looks out at the beach I know that we are seeing two different islands. I think of the minor French noble who, attempting to persuade his uncle to invest in his Sapelo Company in the early days of the French Revolution, described the island as 'the *Eden.*' We sit under a pavilion on the boardwalk, watching her children run back and forth across the hard, flat sand. We are the only people there for an hour, until a tour bus arrives and its passengers disembark with cameras around their necks. It is this isolation, I realise, that birthed the Geechee culture, its unique creole and traditions.

Most days I drive to the Post Office, once a sugar mill, on Long Tabby Road to use the internet. I had been using mobile data until one of the owners came out to tell me the Wi-Fi password. There is no internet at my grandmother's house, and hardly any mobile signal. This is pretty normal: some of the older houses aren't even hooked up to a landline. I park the cart by a wide creek, under the shade of a large saw palmetto tree. I text my friends and send a couple of emails. A crocodile sunbathes on the muddy bank opposite.

When I return to Hogg Hummock in the afternoon, I sit in the house where it's cool and dark. My grandparents and I talk across the kitchen table. My grandmother explains the relationship she has with the people at the marine institute.

'I'll work with them,' she says, 'but I don't trust them. The people from the university say they're protecting the environment, the animals and everything. But we were protecting the environment. It's the state that bought the land and sold it to developers; it's the state that made it so people wanted to sell. They don't see us as part of the island. But we're part of Sapelo too.'

The back door is open. People come and go, some stay a while. We drink sweet iced tea or, as the day wears out, moonshine. An older guest asks me to repeat a few words, and I oblige her, before my grandmother playfully slaps her arm.

'I love to hear her speak the King's English!' says the guest. For a moment, I am bewildered – there hasn't been a king in England while I've been alive.

Visitors to the island say that life moves at a slow, leisurely pace here. The hours drip like honey on Sapelo, resistant but sweet. And there's an easiness that marks out the community of Hogg Hummock from the other parts of the island with their ruins, the big house, the marine institute. These areas are palpably marked by a sense of antagonism. The same animosity that exists between the long-time residents and some part-timers has also soured the community's view of the scientists at the marine institute, which is affiliated with the University of Georgia. And the big house, now a guest house for tourists, is symbolic of a past that feels very present to many islanders.

As the night comes in, conversations frequently turn to a 'they'. They are responsible for property taxes rising, they are responsible for the closure of the island's school in 1978, they won't do anything about the lack of public infrastructure on the island – there is no fire station, no medical centre, no curbside garbage pick-up – and they want to buy out the last Saltwater Geechees in Hogg Hummock.

'They want to move us out,' says an uncle, 'so they can move in.'

Others whisper agreement. The names of other islands and towns and cities are invoked as warnings. 'Look what happened to St Simon's after they built the land bridge,' says a cousin. 'Hell, look what's happening to Savannah. Nobody can't afford to live anywhere.'

Sometimes I can't tell if this 'they' is the state or the county, the marine scientists or the tourists. It doesn't really matter – there is always a 'they' on Sapelo; an invisible Other with more control over the material conditions of the residents' lives than they have themselves. Even my grandmother is worried, which worries me, because it's she who always says that nothing can separate us from the island. The land doesn't belong to us, she says, we belong to the land.

3 TURTLE ISLAND

At sea, a bird is one of the first signs of land. A sailor first sees the colour green, like a floating garden, before realising that it has roots. Today, virtually no one approaches Sapelo from the open ocean. The ferry navigates inland waterways, and otherwise the island is only accessible by private boat or aircraft. But in the nineteenth century, even after the importation of slaves was outlawed, ships would secretly dock in the Sea Islands, guided by Sapelo's lighthouse, to traffic in human beings.

It's difficult to understand what it meant to see the island for the first time at such a distance, after a months-long journey in a cargo hold, shimmering on the water like a dream or perhaps like purgatory, white pelicans and roseate spoonbills flying and calling overhead.

The creation myths of various indigenous nations, from the Cherokee to the Iroquois to the Ojibwe, credit a turtle with creating landmass on an oceanic Earth, or shepherding the people to dry land after a great flood. This is why the North American continent is sometimes called Turtle Island. When the Spanish reached Sapalaw, which is the Guale name for the island, in the sixteenth century, they named it Zapala and set up a mission in honour of San José. A century later, the fruit trees that the missionaries had planted were still growing, but the mission was abandoned. England was expanding its territories along the coast as the influence of other European powers waned in the region, and in 1733, Georgia was declared a British colony.

Yet while the Spanish and the English had first reached the island by travelling over land then crossing the river, it was the sailors and the slaves, if they were not confined to the hold, who would have been the first to see, in maybe hundreds of years, that verdant mirage. The last known slave ship to arrive in the Sea Islands from Africa landed at Jekyll Island in 1858, and it was the penultimate ship to cross the Middle Passage to what European settlers had, by then, named the United States of America.

***

The air off the sea tastes salt-sharp. The island, retreating in the ferry's wake, resembles a turtle's back. It's seven in the morning, and the sky is pale. Dolphins reappear intermittently alongside the ferry. A small group of school children talk excitedly among themselves, their voices occasionally rising to a collective shout before an elder chides them to quiet down. In the eighties and nineties, when my older brothers and sisters were elementary school-age, this group would have been much bigger. Now it is down to a handful – the children and grandchildren of Hogg Hummock's few remaining black residents. When the Katie Underwood arrives in Meridian, the yellow school bus is waiting. This is its first stop. It will take the children to school in the nearby city of Darien.

***

Clashes between the Spanish, the French and the English in the seventeenth and eighteenth centuries – as they tried to secure the strategic position that the barrier islands offered – disrupted wildlife and natural environments, and decimated and dislocated indigenous tribes. With the native populations cleared from the southeast, the land became a resource for planters and settlers. In what would become the city of Darien, these settlers included a group of Scottish Highlanders, who had travelled to Georgia in the early eighteenth century at the invitation of James Oglethorpe, the colony's founder. To build Darien, the Highlanders set about the 'heavy labor of clearing land out of a wilderness.' Among this group was John McIntosh, after whom the county is now named.

The Darien settlers had left behind a Scotland where clan chieftains were beginning to view themselves not as patriarchs but as landlords, with the power to forcibly evict their tenants – their clansmen – at will, moving them to other parts of the Highlands region or even expelling them entirely. In 1883, Alexander Mackenzie wrote of the 'harsh, cruel and inhuman conduct' used to turn out entire families from their homes. Playing the bagpipe and wearing plaid were outlawed, accelerating expulsions and emigrations by criminalising expressions of Scottish culture.

As in the American southeast, the expansionist and economic imperatives of the British Empire saw large tracts of land in Scotland consolidated into private ownership, while thousands of people were separated from their ancestral homes and redirected to towns and cities at the height of industrialisation. These removals would later become known as the Highland Clearances.

***

My grandmother and I are going shopping. We drive to the grocery store to buy fresh food, and then onwards to an outlet mall for a gift for a cousin's birthday. There is a sense of urgency to the morning: we have to make it back to the dock in Meridian before twelve, or else wait until the afternoon for the last ferry. No errand is easy when you live on Sapelo. Having been raised in rural Wales, I am familiar with the day-long errands that would take only fifteen minutes in a large city.

In the old days, when my grandmother was a little girl, it would have been an event to make a trip to Darien or Brunswick. The island had grocers and butchers and a general store, and most families grew some crops and could make and mend their own clothes, or place an order from the Sears catalogue if they wanted. But today the uneven development and inadequate infrastructure on Sapelo means that islanders aren't as self-sufficient as they once were.

My grandmother mourns the closure of the school, in particular. After the school went, she says, so did everything and everyone else. The young families sold up and moved away, to save their children the convoluted commute across the water. The elders left to join their kids. With them went so many of the people who knew how to weave a basket out of sweetgrass, the people who knew how to cast the seine net, the people who knew how to lead a group of others in a shout.

Without people, my grandmother says, the culture starts to falter and fade. There's no one to pass it down and no one for it to be passed down to.

***

Before it was owned by an empire, Sapelo was inhabited by the Guale people, and later the Muscogee Creek. An ancient shell mound on the north end of the island attests to their presence. In the mid-eighteenth century, Sapelo was owned by Mary Musgrove, whose Creek name was Coosaponakeesa. Her father was a white trader from Charleston in South Carolina, and her mother a Creek woman from Coweta Town in what is now Coweta County, Georgia. Musgrove was an interpreter and intermediary for James Oglethorpe, and was herself a slave owner. Although a Lower Creek chief had granted her ownership of Sapelo, Ossabaw and St Catherine's, the British Crown forced her to cede the former two islands.

A series of slave owners ran plantations on Sapelo throughout the latter part of the seventeenth century. By the middle of the eighteenth, Thomas Spalding owned almost all of the land on Sapelo. By this time, coastal Georgia had long been settled and occupied by Europeans, but there was still substantial territory belonging to the Creek Nation to the west. In 1825, a group of chiefs including William McIntosh, a descendant of the Darien settler John McIntosh, signed the Treaty of Indian Springs. The treaty ceded all remaining Creek land in Georgia, as well as three million acres in Alabama, to the federal government. This was a capital crime. The Creek Nation Council ordered the chiefs' executions.

The Trail of Tears stretched west from North America's southeast to Oklahoma, which the government had designated 'Indian Territory' in 1834. Thousands of Native Americans were forcibly removed from their homes, including some of McIntosh's descendants. The Americans had realised, as had the British, the Spanish and the French, that the incorporation of an indigenous elite into the economic ranks of a settler society could destabilise entire groups, and prepare the ground for large-scale depopulations that would make land and natural resources available for industrial exploitation.

In the Highlands, the transformation of clan chiefs into landlords precipitated the slow death of the formal clan system and the fracturing of communities that had lived and worked the same land for hundreds of years. In the American southeast, the seizure and ceding of sovereign land preceded the forcible removal of whole peoples. These displacements, those that preceded the Trail of Tears and those that came after, would create the island of Sapelo, the colony of Georgia, the United States of America. From the Atlantic to the Pacific, Turtle Island is a country built by clearances.

4 DAYCLEAN

We call the morning 'dayclean' in Gullah. The word describes, I think, the way the air feels in the morning. It is easier to move, to think. The day before I am to leave, I drive to the marine institute. I do not go inside. The building is two storeys tall, with a terracotta roof. It used to be a dairy barn, belonging originally to the Reynolds estate. A fountain with a turkey as its centrepiece sits in front of the main entrance.

Within walking distance is the big house. The air of decline that I feel in Hogg Hummock is stilled here. Everything seems immortal, fixed in both time and place. The front gardens are neat and pretty, with Greco-Roman imitation statues arranged on the lawn. There is a stone fountain with a tiled, aqua blue interior and no water. At its centre, a woman on her knees raises her hands to the sky.

There is almost no trace of the rows of slave dwellings that would have been a stone's throw from the main house. If Hogg Hummock is one day empty, this is what will be preserved of Sapelo's past: the white statues, the short grass, the grand archways and ballrooms. Nothing of the people who named the island or those who worked its fields. Nothing of their lives.

***

After the Civil War, descendants of the slaves who worked on Spalding's plantation bought parcels of land on Sapelo for the black families who lived there. The William Hillery Company, a partnership of freedmen, pooled their financial resources to secure, for a while, the autonomy of the Geechee people on the island.

Sapelo's communities of black freedmen flourished into the early twentieth century. A future where Sapelo could be owned by its people was foreclosed, however, when Howard Coffin bought most of the island in 1912. Coffin sold the land to Richard J. Reynolds in 1934. But Coffin had not owned the black communities, so Reynolds set about the work of consolidating the rest of the island into his estate, buying out black landowners until he owned all but the 434 acres that make up Hogg Hummock. Then, in 1976, Reynolds' widow sold the island to the state of Georgia.

***

My grandmother has three dreams for the island. The first is for the crumbling plantation ruins up at Chocolate. She extends her arm wide, passing it over the field: a model village, to attract tourists who want to know about the history. The second, for Hogg Hummock: a new school, an expanded store. Real homes. The third, for Sapelo: the state to return the island, in its entirety, over to the slave descendants both on the island and on the mainland.

When my grandmother asks if I would ever move to the island (because we need young people, she says), and when I say yes, we are talking about a future where her dreams have prevailed, and every corner of the island is alive with Geechee people. Sapelo would have to be owned by us, she says, for any of it to last. Every oak tree, every pine, every beach and field and river. The land would have to be ours and we'd have to know to hold onto it.

NEIL GOWER

From Light and Language and Tides

November 1968, 9.20am; Romilly Infants School Hall, Barry.

The radio is the size of a fridge. The only feature on its wooden face is a round mesh speaker. Beyond the tall windows of the hall, beyond the town and Barry Island, the Bristol Channel is swollen and metallic around the islands of Flat Holm and Steep Holm. In the dock that separates town from Island, a crane is unloading a Geest banana boat fresh from the West Indies, its sleek white lines at odds in the Glamorgan gloom. Every eight-year-old in the hall has heard the rumours that each crate of bananas contains at least one tarantula, perfectly capable of finding its way to lurk under the toilet seats of Barry. Restless daps squeak on the parquet as Mrs Weaving leans behind the cabinet, turning the dial in search of BBC Schools' 'Music and Movement'. Suddenly, out of the crackle and pop, a voice emerges with startling clarity: '*Do you know the way to San Jose?*'. It vanishes into Mrs Weaving's frown as she continues her search. One boy is smiling though, as if in receipt of a message from beyond. He is enjoying the brief, comforting knowledge that he's probably the only child there who does know the way.

***

November 2019, 8.25am; Holmfirth Bus Station.

I am waiting for Simon Armitage. It is late autumn, a time of floods and first frosts. The river is in full, peaty spate. I stamp my feet, partly for warmth and partly to alleviate a low-level anxiety. How will a Poet Laureate arrive? On horseback, to a fanfare? Accompanied by a harlequin? The truth reveals itself on the dot of 8.30 in the form of an unmistakable fringe at the wheel of a grey Honda. After introductions that feel almost competitively mild-mannered, we begin the long climb north out of Holmfirth onto moorland, towards Marsden. As someone who recently enjoyed his first modest success in the Welsh Poetry Competition, and finding himself with the Poet Laureate captive, I am making the inevitable mental calculation: when best to hit him with 'I write a bit of poetry myself...'.

The plan is for us to spend a day in and around Simon's hometown, visiting locations that have inspired or appeared in his poetry. I will map them for the endpapers of his forthcoming anthology *Magnetic Field*, which will contain all of his poems that are set in, or refer to, the town and its surroundings. The depth of Simon's connection with this place is a potent alchemy of prolonged intimacy and a geography degree, within which childhood scrapes under the immense brick flanks of Bank Bottom Mill fuse with an understanding of the Marsdenian Age's significance in late Carboniferous sandstone deposits.

It is immediately clear that Simon has a heightened sensitivity to the authority and poetry inherent in maps: something that has also enthralled me since my childhood. I would pore over atlases, thrilling to the colours, fonts and names. It was all simultaneously so psychedelic, yet so infallibly measured. The discovery that the Bristol Channel outside our school window in Barry has the second highest tidal range in the world[1] gave me a sense of pride that was only intensified by the sight of my own name – G O W E R – set into the map beside it like five jewels, exquisitely spaced across a peninsula. It may have been this that attuned me to the music of place-names and their attendant anticipated arrivals. I would thrill to the sounds of Winnipeg and Wagga Wagga. And as for the discovery that there was really a town in Uruguay called Fray Bentos...

Our shared cartographic sensibilities have engaged before the Honda is in fifth gear. We identify the importance of integrating the maps with the poetry, and we agree that two maps will be required – one for town, one for moor. We want them to serve a deeper function than simply marking locations. The maps will need to work as a cartographic biography, plotting a journey into adulthood and the creative development of an artist.

We very briefly consider writing the title of each poem in its place on the map, but see instantly that this will be unfeasible, given, for example, the concentration of poems in and around the house on Mount Road where he grew up (some with titles as unwieldy as 'A Few Don'ts About Decoration') and the fact that some poems contain more than one location and will need to appear several times. Numbering immediately feels right, its hint at increment echoing the subtext of creative development. They will be maps as an index to a life. The poems' page

---

[1] The Bay of Fundy in Nova Scotia, since you ask.

numbers will be inlaid into the topography, affording them the cool infallibility of numbers indicating depths and altitude on maritime charts and relief maps. We are getting on famously. I decide to hold fire on mentioning my own poetry.

Work proper begins on Mount Road, which rises steeply out of town, its foot opposite the churchyard, leading ultimately to lofty and windswept Pule Hill. The house is an end-of-terrace, tellingly suspended between town and moor. It offered sufficient altitude for the young Armitage to see the 'town as amphitheatre', yet still cleaves to the bosom of Marsden for protection from the vast moors and Pennines that loom beyond. From this neat wedge of stone, privet and picture-window he cultivated the unassuming omnipotence that characterises many of his observations: watching, waiting for the glint of a cufflink as his father returns from a function, or glimpsing his mother down in the town, crossing a street with a purse in her fist. There is a strong sense of existing between the two worlds of town and moor. In one poem, the two threaten to collide disastrously when a group of boys rolls a huge, abandoned tractor tyre from the high moor down towards the town. The tyre gains momentum towards imagined catastrophes. In another, the death of a philandering motorist cautions against trifling with the landscape's capricious affections.

All towns are defined as much by their surroundings as by their streets. Marsden's relationship with its landscape is an angular harmony between what has been allowed to encroach and serve the town, and what is held back. Even compiling the list of locations to be featured on the maps proved a poetic testament to human interaction with its hinterland: First Quarry, Fretwell's Farm, Second Quarry, Wool Clough, Tunnel End Reservoir.

The scale and texture of the town's setting reminds me immediately of the Rhondda Valley where my own roots lie. It induces an identical sympathy for a landscape harnessed and invaded by the Industrial Revolution. The Rhondda has its mineshafts and networks of plundered seams; Marsden has its reservoirs and the Standedge Tunnels ushering the Huddersfield Narrow Canal and the Leeds–Manchester Trans-Pennine rail link beneath Pule Hill and the moors, to emerge over five kilometres away in Diggle, Lancashire.

This feeling of vast elements restrained is best exemplified by the flight of four reservoirs that rise above Marsden to the south: Butterley, Blakeley, Wessenden and Wessenden Head. As I plotted them on the map alongside Simon's poems, their distinctive forms caught my attention. They brought to mind Mary Ruefle's observation about how poetry itself takes shape:

I think it is easier to talk about the end of a poem than it is to talk about the beginning. Because the poem ends on the page, but it begins off the page, it begins in the mind.

Each reservoir is the product of water trickling and filtering through peat, soil, rock; a poem has the same indeterminate catchment. Its origins are far-flung, disparate and impossible to identify. It is the crystallisation in printed form of droplets that have been filtered – often subliminally – by the poet's emotional and psychological geology.

The four reservoirs sit there on the map: each shape defined by the line of equilibrium between what feeds in and what confines it. The outline of each one begins to resemble a poem on the page. The four forms are organic, except for the lower, Marsden-ward edge of each, which is flat and guillotine-straight – a dam, like a perfect closing line, giving poignant form to all that precedes it. I see poetry for the first time as resembling arrested water; the rippled surface of something 'within' the page, complex in its anatomy and sources; a dimensional entity simultaneously part of *and* discrete from its surroundings.

There is an expansive rawness to the landscape around Marsden. It is a nakedness, but not one that is coy or vulnerable. It is as challengingly confident in its own rawness as the slabs of pigment on a Lucien Freud haunch. I am transported once more to the Rhondda, in particular to the famously perfect cirque above Blaenrhondda. My father would always point it out, raising his voice as the Ford Anglia whined up Rhigos Mountain Road in second gear. This would trigger the same sense of pride as the Bristol Channel tides. I would generally celebrate these moments when the world around me found traction with my atlas by running to its pages and copying the maps. I rendered coastlines, noting and emulating the differing fonts and trying to match the subtlety of the graded colours that represented altitude and fathoms. Having only cheap pencils and poster paints at my disposal, this was generally a doomed and frustrating enterprise, but something in the process provided an atavistic, physical thrill. I swear that, on occasion when a pleasing combination of word and colour appeared, my pelvis would hum.

Thus enthused, I would allow the interaction between my own environment and my passions for maps and mark-making to fuel a wider wanderlust. I would watch the orange aircraft of Cambrian Airways skimming in over the cliffs and viaduct at Porthkerry, still hot – so it seemed to me – from Alicante or Rimini, to land at Rhoose (since exalted to Rhoose Cardiff International). I would sometimes cycle to the airport to watch the planes come and go. Once a year, my father would drive me over the Severn Bridge, all the way down the M4 to spend a day at Heathrow, where more exotic creatures were available – 747s with names like *Emperor Rajendra Chola*; with Pan Am's globe or Singapore Airlines' (then new) kris bird adorning their tailfins. It was all a perfect marriage of graphics and geography. Once or twice, when we arrived early enough, we got to see Concorde take off, all gonzo nose and primal noise. (Concorde also passed over our house, and the sonic boom as it decelerated over the Bristol Channel would regularly rattle my mother's glass animals.) In Terminal 3 the destinations tumbling across the departure boards would quicken my pulse. It was as if the gazetteer in one of my atlases was flickering into life.

I could sense a certainty in the interaction between words and shapes on a map. A map has a truth: it is faithful to something beyond itself, an elsewhere. A poem has a similar quality: it is an exactingly compiled entity, devised to convey as accurately as possible an experience or moment, whether in a spirit of guiding others who might pass the same way or of recording knowledge. Identifying when a poem is finished is not an exact science. In most cases they lurch and fizzle to completion through sporadic and increasingly tiny edits, often reversals of the preceding one. However, every now and then – it has happened to me twice – at the insertion of a crucial word or the judicious fracture of a line, the whole poem will shimmer and click into order on the screen, rather like a departure board updating itself to a new truth. The sudden percolation of these visions surprises me. It is as though finding myself in the Poet Laureate's passenger seat discussing maps and poetry has triggered some kind of short-circuit between my childhood and the present.

We cover a lot of town and moor before dusk – dams, bridleways, towpaths, alleys; we cross and recross contour lines both in the Honda and on foot. Simon takes the photographs that will appear in *Magnetic Field*, while I take notes and make sketches as he explains the significance of each location. These launch digressions into compared childhoods, families, creative processes... He snaps Bank Bottom Mill from Mount Road. I scribble, and I am suddenly back in Ogmore Vale sketching Wyndham Colliery winding gear and banks of terraced houses.

'10 minutes, the whole thing, mark up your three points and start from there, no rubbing out...'

The voice isn't Simon's – it belongs to Tom Hutchinson, the passionate and visionary art teacher at Brynteg Comprehensive, Bridgend. On Sundays he would commandeer the growling, bronze school minibus and test its gearbox on sketching expeditions over the Bwlch, or to the breakers' yard at Briton Ferry. He presented us with industrial-scale subjects and scenic grandeur 'to get our eyes and hands fit'. And it was – still is – a kind of fitness, a facility: the energising realisation that your hand is drawing intuitively while your eye is still on the subject. Mr Hutchinson taught me a lot about how to draw, but above all he taught me how to enjoy it, to live it – that it might just be possible to embrace that pelvic hum and run with it into adulthood. The unanticipated glimpses of my own upbringing are brought into even sharper focus when I learn that Simon's wife also grew up in the Rhondda and he tells a rather beautiful – though I suspect apocryphal – story about the lights on the Ferndale Christmas tree.

The longer we talk, and the more of Simon's life and the way it has emerged in his art is plotted across my map, the more I appreciate the profundity of his connection with this place. I also begin to catch glimpses of a new terrain for me to piece together and plot. It is the topography of my own career as a visual artist – and, latterly, poet – which lies between my south Wales childhood and the South Downs where I now live. It strikes me that I have migrated from black to white, exchanging Rhondda coal for Sussex chalk. For many years as an illustrator, devising book jackets and maps, I distilled the words of others into paint. Did I need the clarity of chalklands to release my own words? My voice snags on unexpected emotion as I tell Simon of my gratitude for the two things that have had an infinite capacity to surprise, inspire and sustain me all my life. They are light, and the English language.

We have an appointment at 5pm in St Bartholomew's Church. In a couple of weeks, Simon is due to give his first hometown reading in several years: a fund-raising event for which 400 people have each paid £12. Having sat through unintelligible, echoing services himself over many years he is keen to ensure the sound quality is first-rate. Debate centres around whether he should deliver the poetry from floor level near the 'congregation' through a capricious borrowed PA (set up by two mates of his dad, eager to out-expert each other in the way that only middle-aged men with minimal knowledge can), or via the church's own address system. The latter's sound quality is superior but has two drawbacks: a) it renders him invisible behind the extravagant gold eagle lectern within which the only mic is embedded, and b) the system's legendary tendency to pick up local minicab dispatches mid-sermon. After much experimentation with permutations of jacks, leads and microphones – not to mention jogging up and down the nave to check acoustics for 'the poor sods at the back' – the whole episode proves mightily entertaining but, alas, inconclusive.

A small company adjourns to the pub, comprising Simon, me, his father and the two eager roadies, one of whom introduces himself as Marsden's barber since 1973 (cue another reflexive glance at Simon's fringe). I sit back and enjoy their easy companionship, recalling how many times during the day Simon has been stopped by well-wishers expressing gratitude for a favourite poem or, more significantly to me, putting their part of the world on the map. It is precisely *this* terrain, and the integrity of Simon's connection with it, that I must plot.

I have never mapped a life in poetry before. Today's preparation for doing so has placed me at the centre of a unique triangulation of image, word and place. Their alignment has tilted an unexpected and exacting lens onto my own life as an artist and poet. Simon still inhabits the heart of this place, and belongs to its people. I am left wondering just how intact the connection with my own birthplace is: what propelled my *scurochiaro* transit from black to white?

When I was growing up surrounded by coal, I craved and conjured colour. I chose drawing and painting. I chose maps. I chose all the elsewheres I could find, whether in the pages of my atlas or the lyrics of a Bacharach/David song. Now I find myself living on luminous chalk, I wonder whether my migration out of south Wales was inevitable: ordained perhaps in the cascading stanzas of airport departure boards. The Sussex light is white. White light, by its nature, ensures every colour is at my disposal in its purest form for painting. It enables me to read and compose words with greater clarity. The journey from boy to man has presented me with light and language as a form of currency. Each has an infinite capacity to inspire me. Both touch everyone, and both are relentless: light in its infallibility, language with its malleable intricacies perpetuated only by the necessity of human interaction.

***

1 October 2021; driving from Lewes to Swansea.

Every time I make this journey, I pass both Gatwick and Heathrow airports. The inbound and outbound tailfins low over the motorways still give me a frisson. The Severn Bridge I cross today is a different, more widescreen structure. Its old counterpart that seemed, from the Anglia's rear window, to scrape the sky, looks pale and puny upstream. Far below, the estuary looks as treacherously veined with eddies as ever.

In her song 'Coyote' Joni Mitchell sings of being far from the Bay of Fundy, 'from Appaloosas and eagles and tides'. Every time I hear that line I think of this restless tract of water and feel, alongside the tug of *hiraeth*, a sense of insignificance and awe at the majesty of her lyrics. These emotions are direct echoes of those triggered by the phenomena of tides and the Rhigos cirque when I was a child, that boy with one eye constantly on a white boat in the dock, the Channel and the Somerset coast beyond.

Less than fifteen miles after the bridge and the *Croeso i Gymru* sign, the cliff-face of the Celtic Manor Resort looms high to my right. As I pass, my eye alights as always on the smaller, more elegant building cradled beneath it (recently

133

further obscured by the unsightly, stealth-bomber angles of the new ICC Wales building). Now part of the hotel complex, this was once the Lydia Beynon Maternity Hospital.

It is where I was born.

I see with sudden clarity how my own birthplace has cast an uneasy shadow on every journey to and from the Severn Bridge, on every departure from and arrival in Wales. It is the knowledge that I was born in the very bottom right-hand corner of Wales – and so close to the quickest, most conspicuous way out – that has always compromised my sense of belonging.

From my phone's Bluetooth this time, via the car's stereo, Dionne Warwick poses her question again. I smile, the lyrics in a new focus. She wasn't dreaming of an elsewhere but longing to get home.

JULIE BROMINICKS

The Murmuration

The air is spiced with incense and the wood from which the old town is built. The cry of a hawk lingers and dissolves, and in the park, water lilies cover the lake, their greenness complementing the red footbridge. I have chosen this quiet place because I feel uneasy in cities full of people whose expressions I struggle to interpret, and whose glances I sense but never catch. The university here is predominantly for Japanese trainee teachers. Among them are a few Chinese and Korean students who've been learning Japanese all through school. I'm a Brit on a scholarship, my research will be self-directed, and my Japanese is brand new. I'm apprehensive, but receive a warm welcome.

I buy a bicycle and cruise along the riverbank. The river is channelled by concrete and crossed by many bridges. I cycle to the Super Sento, which has herbs in cloth bags and a steam room where little girls stare at me and obaasan don't. I cycle through rice fields where frogs croak and a boy skips by with a butterfly net. I cycle into wooded hills, where big black butterflies wobble. The trees have even more depth at night. Fireflies float among them like tiny fishing boats. The fireflies rise, float, seem too heavy for the air, and slowly descend.

I cycle to the coast. A crab runs across the path with raised pincers. It is cooler in the evening, and my bike seems to push the air aside, as if it is dense. Moths batter my headlight and insects click in the shrubs.

The warm air turns thick and clammy as spring becomes summer. Clouds creep over the mountains and stay there. Everyone is waiting for the rain. Then one day, a gust of wind knocks over my bike and scatters my shopping across the pavement.

We international students are invited to cultural events. Tea ceremony apprentices pour us bitter green tea, and the Japanese students scream with delight when I make Tanabata sweets with them. Later they warn me that bears are dangerous in Japan, especially when emerging from hibernation. The students are kind, but I am struggling with the language and need time to recover after our meetings. They are also younger than me, so it would feel odd to tag along, and I appreciate from my own experience that supporting a language learner is as exhausting as being one. I sense disappointment but also relief when I begin to decline invitations. But I do go along to a shamisen concert performed by men in kimonos. It is absorbing and beautiful and I can sit in the dark and don't have to speak to anyone.

But I would like to be able to speak, particularly to the people in the old town. I discover a street market there, held on dates with a 3 or an 8 in them, with elderly vendors squatting under faded parasols to sell bunches of vegetables and wild flowers, or perching on stools behind tables bearing fish, seeds or tools. I buy spring onions from a wrinkly obaasan who presses two lettuces into my hands, and coffee from a man boiling water in a jug on a gas ring. I crouch behind some flowerpots to drink it. A gust of wind blows a parasol into the dorayaki stall, and the rains arrive.

The river becomes a brown torrent rising up the concrete banks, and the fields become very green. Obaasan in bonnets tend vegetables, and forage for wayside herbs. Up at the reservoir the air is wet and thick, and shining raindrops roll around on the leaves. In the old town, the wood and paper buildings absorb the moisture. But everything on campus is dripping wet. I slip over in the corridor and some of my clothes go mouldy in the cupboard.

In a gap between downpours, we go to the beach. I teach the students the inflatable globe game – where the person who throws it challenges the person who catches it to find a certain country. They teach me how to play the watermelon game – you tie it up in a plastic bag and bash it, blindfolded, with a stick. Clouds sweep towards sunset. I like the students very much, but I am too stubborn to speak English, and not disciplined or clever enough to fast-track my Japanese. My mistakes make me clumsy and a bit of a nuisance. But I go with them to Noh theatre and melt into the dark. The performers move softly with white-socked feet. A devil zooms backwards through the curtain. I don't want the lights to come back on.

I spend less time trying to join in.

It is still raining. There are mud slides across the country and somewhere a road is washed away. The mountains are wrapped in mist. The rice grows tall and green. The river smells alternately fresh or of bad breath. I cycle up and down it, looking at the little bridges, the heavy wires, the ugly new buildings, the wonky wooden old ones, and the temples. I glimpse a portable golden shrine being carried into a shop.

The rains ease. There is talk of typhoons.

I cycle into the old town to watch the dancing I didn't attend rehearsals for. The international students don't see me. They are part of a massive procession of groups in yukata all doing the same slow swirly dances up the High Street and back. I sit on the ground by two old men squatting at a makeshift bar. The old men don't speak, but I like it there, crouching at the edge. One day I find a quiet temple with lotus flowering in barrels of water. A tiny green frog clings to a stalk and another sits on a leaf. The frogs and I look at each other. One evening I cycle in the dark to a shrine and watch a bank of clouds curl like Hokusai's wave over a crescent moon. Another day I see kindergarten toddlers with straw hats holding onto a rope so as not to get lost, and meet a very tiny boy in the toilets who is reaching his hands up to the dryer, the air of which can only ruffle his hair.

A warm arousing wind begins to stir.

One day I meet a carpenter who explains the forestry situation in Japan and introduces me to some of his friends. I'm excited because they are the kindly-looking, comfortably dressed people I have glimpsed going about their business in a relaxed manner, and I wish they were my friends too. Meanwhile, my research connects me to environmentalists like myself who are keen to share knowledge, and we meet up in various cities. They have their own lives of course, and our meetings don't last long. I co-run a conference in the south. I give the odd presentation, teach a bit, write the occasional article. I get involved with the local Nature School and the local Snow Power project, feel at home there, and almost useful. But I spend most of my time at my desk and am a bit lonely.

A typhoon arrives from Korea and I walk up long streets in the rain. Sheets of it fall from a dark sky, disturbed only by glimmers of light and wallops of wind. One day I just lie on my bed to watch the leaves whip about. The carpenter invites me to his workshop, where a forest of drill-bits is covered in a film of sawdust. I fall a bit in love with him, but I know that loneliness is not a good basis on which to build a relationship. Despite this he falls a bit in love with me too, but says he is messed up at the moment. I don't see much of him, or get to know his friends. Sometimes I glimpse them at the market.

At the Super Sento I wallow in scalding water while wind rushes into my face and shakes the bamboo. At the reservoir the sun is wrapped up in mist and the air, charged with dragonflies and cicada whines, feels electric. In the valley, the old people are loading taro roots into garages and sheds. Ojiisan are operating curious rattling machines and obaasan are harvesting vegetables with their headscarves and aprons wrapped tightly against the wind. Tiny fish live in the rice fields. I follow a path around the fields, between misty trees, and encounter brown frogs. In Mister Donuts I drink milky coffee that makes me feel queasy, and see a man jump out of a taxi to photograph the station from the middle of the road. The taxi reverses very gently into him and the man looks surprised, then smiles and bows.

Autumnal displays appear outside doorways in the old town – tortoises made from leaves and scrubbing brushes, or plastic flowers woven into rope. Everything here is aged and faded but very clean. The wooden stores have almost nothing on their shelves, though I glimpse occasional activity within, like ojiisan cutting up paper in the hanko shop. The pavements are sheltered by gangi-dori – three metres of snow fell on them last winter. One day as I am wandering, a merry old man with gold teeth invites me to the chrysanthemum festival. He organises someone to give me a tour of the exhibits, someone else to show me the temple, a monk to explain all the symbols on his yukata, and a man from local TV to film me eating daikon and tofu. I am grateful to be included, but feel a little rundown. Participating in a conversation requires me to monopolise it, to control the pace, the level and the subject – which is not how I normally converse. The only person I can communicate with easily is the carpenter, who is half-American and bilingual. But he is going through a hard time emotionally and I barely see him, so we just write to each other instead.

I don't go to the student festival.

Sometimes I spend so much time alone I forget how to talk.

I venture into the new part of town and drink expensive coffee at a department store while fashionably dressed customers glance at me with apparent disdain, then away. I prefer the old town, though it is in a dark mood. My bike tumbles over while I drink hot tea in a little café. A woman in a beret leaves, a man in a suit nods. I try and understand the old people's gossip. Pickles... kids... TV... Naoetsu Station... twenty years ago – they are just loose words on the run. I cycle slowly down the wooden streets and spy two women in yukata sweeping a courtyard with grass brooms behind open gates. Seeing me watching, another woman tells me the place is a traditional izakaya and that I should bring my friends. But I have no friends.

I head for the mountains.

They are covered with spiky trees and smoky mist. I circumnavigate yellow fields around which rivers babble, and watch harvested rice shoot into paper sacks. I follow a road to a shrine where a cola can has been left as an offering. A tanuki shuffles into the trees. A fat yellow moon rises. Daikon are drying outside the windows of wooden houses now, and at the Nature School, an ojiisan demonstrates how to shake kaki off the trees and gather them so as not to tempt bears. He shows us claw marks on the trunk and tells the children that he ate the bear that made them. The meat was tough, he says. He tells me that the obaasan tell a story about me cycling through the villages, which is funny, because I'd not seen anyone watching.

The villagers are making small preparations, constructing bamboo wigwams to protect trees and shrubs from snow. The sky over the 7-11 is yellow, with dark clouds storming across it. In the Super Sento, wrinkled women draped over a rock are chatting to each other, but they don't seem to notice me. The sky becomes a flimsy white piece of paper onto which mountains and trees made from bits of bark and beans and seeds have been glued like a kindergarten picture. The air is dry and cold. Clouds squat on the mountains like dirty great futons. The trees seem to be waiting for something. In the afternoons after school, the roads are full of kids on bikes, dreaming and nearly crashing. At dusk, cars speed along under purple clouds. One evening, I stop my bike so suddenly to watch obaasan in headscarves and aprons loading greens into a truck that a woman pedalling a tricycle with a basket full of leeks is forced to look straight at me.

I visit every shrine. I follow paths into woods that smell of wet earth, and climb onto a ridge to see mountains stacked to the horizon below masses of black cloud. The clouds become cold mist that spits ice. I take a different route downhill, and come to a woman scrubbing daikon in a bucket while a man smokes a cigarette. The woman digs out two daikon as a gift and the man wraps them in newspaper. I cycle down the coast and get caught up in a convoy of cement trucks and their diesel exhaust. The bundled-up labourers in the trucks shout hello and laugh, and we overtake each other till I leave them on a downhill. The hills are brown and mottled like old cardigans. I cycle under a hawk, see soft white feathers, the direction of its beak, and feel like crying.

I love this place, and these people.

At night, the old town is dark except for a few lights reflected in the rain. Streets disappear into a perspective of dripping wires and gangi-dori. The old town, with its scent of red pine, is like an abandoned piece of antique furniture with quiet sliding drawers and grainy gold lustre, full of rainy temples, and dignified folded people slipping into shadows behind mysterious doors. But it is a magic box and I can't get in. The carpenter and I watch salmon struggle upriver and a frog creep over stones. Mist mutes red leaves. They fall into the water. But it is no good.

I am cycling against the wind. I do not belong.

The wind changes and blows from inland. A crow swings on a wire, roads glower, and the rain enhances bruised hues in collapsing vegetation. The trains are stuffy now the heated seats have been turned on, but there is not enough space to take off my jacket. Everyone's knees almost touch but nobody speaks, nor looks at each other. The first thunderstorm of winter cracks and shakes various things in my room. On campus the trees are naked. The ground is thick with smashed orange leaves which also fill the bicycle baskets and stick to the bike frames and wheels. I work all night in the kenkyushitsu while cars on campus are smothered in icy slush. Thunder rattles the building and a student is asleep in the corridor. I leave when the sky looks like yoghurt. My armpits smell sour. My mouth tastes like trains. So I cycle to the sea. It heaves in brown hills full of weed and twigs. And I cycle to temples where the wind, and the light on the sea, is thrilling, and I watch torn clouds and indigo mountains bleed into the battered industrial coast, and I see that even the telegraph wires and concrete and chimneys and traffic lights look magical and wild from here. The landscape is like paint on glass left out in the rain. I cycle to the beach and sit on driftwood among lightbulbs washed up from the squid boats. Behind the ramshackle houses the first snow is crisp on the peaks. At the Super Sento the women look quietly at the mountains getting dark, with just their heads above water.

An inch of snow has fallen. The inches increase as the snow folds over solid things. I stand barefoot in snow on the beach while crows peck at walnuts in the jetsam. But then the snow turns to wallpaper paste and the sky becomes black. Slush fills the dying rice fields. A man and woman, knee-deep in it, haul muddy daikon into a truck. It is not like last year. There has not even been enough snow yet to open the ski-jos. The campus crows croak and gather as if they have knowledge about this inky damp.

The sky is empty. It's all emptying.

There are fewer stalls at the market. I buy taro, konyaku, dorayaki, and watch people moving quietly through the rain. The coffee vendor is laughing with a man who disappears when I approach. The coffee vendor looks embarrassed and says, 'I hear you ate some daikon?' I love the old town, but it eludes me.

Next, I misunderstand the bonenkai. My speech is about how kind everyone has been to me over the course of the year. Then I realise everyone else's speech is about their hopes for the new year to come. It is the same at the Nature School and the Snow Power project, where I bumble along. I join a Snow Power expedition, assuming that it's headed to an energy scheme, and find myself eating tempura with a fierce ex-monk sinking vast quantities of warm sake while young men in suits pour me beer. Everyone is beautifully kind, but I'm losing my personality. I don't know how to do the things that make me who I am – switch to a green electricity tariff or explain to the campus shop staff why I'd rather they didn't shrink-wrap my bananas. I can't think of a single benefit to society or the environment that justifies my presence here – it feels like I'm only taking, and I realise that loneliness has less to do with the extent you are welcomed into society than with your ability to contribute to it.

The carpenter says he wants to love me but that he has another girlfriend for now.

The sky is a grey sheet of paper.

In the kenkyushitsu I am thinking that the clouds look interesting, but when the students come in they pull down the blinds, so I leave. I head for the Super Sento, and sit in the central bath. Gusts chase bamboo shadows over the walls. They blow puffs of steam about, and yellow and blue rings float over the water into which my tears drop. An old woman with slack stomach and breasts climbs in, mutters something about the wind, and departs. Colour drains from the sky. The water becomes troubled and erupts into tiny black waves. A thunder clap is followed by sharp spits of rain. I imagine staying in the bath forever and the seasons rolling over me.

The temple lotus are dead and broken, and the market is almost completely battened down now, save for a long queue at the dorayaki stall. Fish are slapped onto tables, full of a deep dark coldness. I take the path to the ridge where there is scat and a smell of fox. A snowy blue range floats above me, and beyond still are higher, whiter mountains. A crow call hangs in the air, where I too, seem to be floating. But one day the mountains disappear and hard white snow falls and smashes into powder with such energy I return to the ridge. I recognise the trees. They are white cathedrals. This is what we were waiting for, they tell me. Above the treeline there are tracks where the animals have been; hoof and claw prints criss-crossing the snow, and bear tracks too. Snow tumbles sparkling into my boots. Light flashes round the valley. Powder drifts. Sky and snow and fields conspire in a dazzling white-out.

I carry on at the edge of things, where I belong. I allow myself to be dressed in a musty kimono by two old women – yanked and squeezed and pegged and stuffed with rags and wadding so I feel like a mattress. And when the snow melts I go for a bike ride and get lost on long roads of uncertain symmetry, winding up in the café where the old people are still gossiping and a different salaryman with a furrowed brow is smoking alone, and I look out at the wet road, the karaoke parlour, McDonalds and a big carpark. My friends the mountains are barely visible from here but it's okay because I can imagine myself up there, breathing their cold air, feeling their silence.

When errands take me to Tokyo I remember that I didn't used to like the anonymity of city crowds, and smile, because I don't seem to mind any more. I travel there by night bus, with sodium lights disturbing the curtains. When I arrive it is still dark and just half the neon is lit. Only a few figures hurry through the streets. Drivers yawn in parked taxis, and a man sweeping the gutter is diminished by the empty and enormous expressway. I wait for morning in McDonalds. People are asleep at plastic tables and one woman has put a yellow scarf over her head. When a crowd of shouting drunk kids arrives, I wait in the station instead.

Down there in the subway, dozens of homeless people are sleeping neatly on cardboard, facing the walls or reclining against pillars and chatting quietly. The mood is calm and I, too, feel relaxed and sit down. But suddenly, the homeless people begin to move, and I can't at first fathom why. I don't understand why the sleepers rise as one, fold their cardboard with quiet efficiency, take one step back and lean against the walls, because I haven't yet noticed the gentle vibration. I don't recognise the gradual swelling of sound or rationalise what it is. A distant white noise builds and crackles, till at last I can identify the swishing of suits and clacking of heels and suddenly a tsunami of commuters come running round the corner, skidding in their race to the platforms, a great, wild, silent roar. The flowing and parting murmuration swirls and regroups like Noh theatre players before slowing to a swift glide. I am transfixed by the beautiful silent people hurrying past, who the homeless people, still standing with their backs to the walls, are regarding with amusement. And then something strange begins to happen: I too, am being watched. I feel the homeless people turn their gazes onto me and our eyes connect. Unabashed they are watching *me*, seeking *my* reaction. Their eyes find mine and, recognising something, they don't look away.

E. E. RHODES

All Among the Saints

I am six years old, solemn and stubborn, in pigtails and my favourite red mackintosh and matching waterproof hat. I ask my mum if one trip to Rome counts as three to Bardsey. She frowns, suspicious of anything that hints at blasphemy, and fiddles with the knot that ties her scarf firmly under her chin. She says she'll find someone to ask.

The day on Bardsey Island is crammed with interest, what with the seal colony, the bones of 20,000 saints, the crumbling abbey. There is one excitement after the other, and it is only late that evening, when I am tucked up on the makeshift cushion bed under the table of the rented caravan, that I remember she didn't get me an answer. But then the next day, amid the thrill of Aberdaron and our very first summer holiday, I forget all about it again.

A few weeks later, our parish priest nods as my mum asks him the question. Father Wilfred is elderly, bewhiskered, known for his gentle ways and his generosity with boiled sweets. He bends, looks into my face and asks if I know what question the pilgrimage of life is trying to answer. I shake my head. He smiles and explains that its purpose is to establish the weight of the heart. It is not bad as answers go, even if I only smile back in reply. When I tell my friends at school it cements our view of him as someone who takes us seriously.

***

Fifteen years later, my mum calls to tell me Father Wilfred has died. The funeral sorrows are muted by the soft sway of monastic habits and the quavered chanting of his fading order. Mum gives me a couple of mass cards with his picture on and tells me that he often asked if I'd visited Bardsey again. I slip the cards into the back of a guide to north Wales and the Llŷn Peninsular, with a chapter on Bardsey.

Four of my friends have recently embarked on Vicar School. Over a late-night kitchen conversation I mention the old priest and we argue about the pilgrim route across north Wales, and possible answers to his question. The only solution is to try it, so the possibility becomes reality. Some other friends are interested too, and the number of potential pilgrims grows, but then a twenty-mile practice walk over a long weekend planes us down to a sensible six. We confirm a date late the following spring, a last chance to do something as a group, before work and life and responsibilities take over.

All of us are experienced campers and walkers. But the following May, over a two-week walk we ambitiously telescope into ten days, we proceed to get lost, lose a pack, miss a crucial bus connection, get flooded out and witness a burglary. After twelve days we finally pitch up at the beach I stood on when I was six, nearly three days late for the boat we had arranged to meet. None of us can wait for the next launch, so we agree that we should make time to try this again.

***

Quarter of a century passes. One day I am dusting off an unlabelled cardboard box I haven't opened during any of the last few house moves. It's full of notebooks, leaflets, maps. I shake open a cobwebbed guide book and find the pictures of Father Wilfred.

I read one of the makeshift diaries I made twenty-five years earlier, amused by my inventorying of satisfactions. It's a habit I picked up from my grandmother – unexpected fragments penned in the margins of recipe books, calendars, and paperback novels. I flip the pages, rediscovering waymarks and sights, distances walked, meals eaten, the places we slept each night. There are a few postcards. The colours are fading, time leaching them of browns and reds until they merge into impressionist yellows, blues and greens.

I scan the scathing notes I made about my friends: Chris' commitment to an 'authentic' route; the way Sam claimed she glued us together; Sandy's passive aggressive scoffing at the pieties of the three priests in training; Thomas' overstuffed too-heavy pack; Mark's obsession with a small leather-bound volume of Celtic saints. And how they complained I was slow: too distracted by the vernacular of the buildings; the honesty boxes that dotted the route; the flowers along the hedgerows; the slate fences marking the margins like grey-rotted molars in a decadent jaw.

I have spoken to none of them for twenty years.

The three men are still priests, all of them vicars in charge of frantic urban parishes. Sandy is busy being a wife and mom in Calgary, and Sam is drowning in the social media of a charity in London. I find them just by Googling their names. I message each of them and wait. I don't recognise any of their faces. All of us are pixelated by Skype, drained of the enthusiasms that made us pilgrims together. I hold up a picture of Father Wilfred and ask if there is any appetite for another go, to see if we can make it onto the island this time, and finally answer the old questions. It kindles a small spark.

We begin to make plans. Accommodation. Luggage. Gear. A guide that describes the newly official route, close to the one we walked. But gradually, the weariness and a wariness of the time commitment tells. Sandy is the first to drop out, then Sam, then Chris and Thomas in emails so similar they must have privately agreed on what to say. I write expansive emails begging them to come. Mark messages me a week before we're supposed to leave. Apologising. I'm still that stubborn six-year-old. I don't tell my partner I'll walk alone; I just stamp and address two jiffy bags containing treats and extra books and tell him exactly when to post them so I can pick them up en route.

On the train I lean forward in my seat, paying attention, pulling myself into the story of pilgrimage that I have convinced myself to tell over 140 miles. I've got twelve days before I must be back at work. My right knee twangs as if in anticipation. I shift in my seat and thread both ankles round the table leg of the cramping Sprinter train. When I arrive at Basingwerk Abbey I write five postcards with a picture of Saint Winefride's Well on the front, and stick a gold star on each one, as if to say, 'I am here'. I pop them into the first postbox I see. Father Wilfred might say it was a start.

The first night, I stay in a chocolate-boxy bed and breakfast, tiptoeing around the rules and easing myself into the kind of interactions I expect to populate my days. Mrs Jones is dressed in Sunday best on a Monday afternoon, but with a nylon tabard over the top. She's a woman settled and certain of her choices. The tabard is a hypnotising hippy pattern of brown, yellow and lime. She has a special visitors' book for pilgrims. I ask her if she's done the walk herself and she laughs, saying she wouldn't dream of it. She went to the island when she was a child, mind.

This must be true for thousands of holidaymakers: a visit to the Llŷn peninsula incomplete without a tummy-lurching trip to the island to which it points. A couple of hours to take in the sights – the ruins, the mountain, the shop, the fields, the enduring silences – all the while being dive-bombed by seabirds. Mrs Jones' trip was from her Llandudno primary school. She smiles at something vivid in her mind's eye, and offers to make me a flask of tea in the morning.

She waves me off just after eight, saying she hopes I make it. She wipes her hands on another swirl-patterned tabard, this one in avocado and pink, and in the sunshine I realise she is probably younger than me.

Over these first few days I make good time. Nothing is different and everything is changed by the absence of the others. Buzzards still mew urgently, owls still ghost-wing across the night, blackbirds still wake me at dawn. I am buoyed by the scent of gorse and hawthorn, and the early hedgerow glory. The occasional whiffs of salt in the air, of warm stone, of dirt and dust, are all familiar. I learned the language of buildings and walking and birdsong long ago. The whispering woods and water feel as welcome as long-anticipated good news.

The days have their own litany – wake up, eat, walk, shop, walk some more, eat, sleep, repeat. There is little to distinguish between them except for the capricious seasonal oscillation between brittle sunshine and slanting rain, and the distinctive pilgrim ink-stamps I sometimes remember to collect in the back of my guidebook. My notebook becomes more grounded in the moment; there is just the here, the now, and the next damp-drying step in front. I get along fast and ask my notebook if I am more suited to the peace and pace of the solitary walker than the gossipy plod of the pilgrim.

The waymarked path along back-roads and tracks is busy. Everyone I meet is friendly enough. I stop in a grocer's with a gilt-painted window to buy milk and ask about the pilgrim traffic. The woman behind the counter is 1950s-glamorous, hair piled high, grey eyes behind violet winged glasses on a long rhinestone chain. She makes a face, tension creasing the corners of her mouth, and leans forward conspiratorially. She says it hasn't been the same since the route was officialised. Especially busy since it featured in a Sunday supplement and went viral on some travel writer's blog. She leans even tighter, nodding, and whispers that everyone knows last year's must-have novel is set on a fictitious version of the island.

I find myself nodding back, telling her about life on a canal boat and that the curious eyes peering in through our windows made me feel zooed. She glances at my rucksack and I apologise quickly. You're all right, she tells me, but you should be careful. A woman alone? She doesn't finish and I'm left wondering if she means in general or specifically. She turns to the couple behind me, who are patiently waiting to pay for their full basket of shopping, and I forget to thank her.

That evening I reach the church where twenty-five years earlier we slept on the vestry floor. I don't think it is the same vicar, but if it is, the elbow-patch sweater that hides his dog collar camouflages him now, as then. He whisks me round the font with the pagan symbols, the woodwormed hammerwork beams, and the subdued jewel colours of the old stained glass. He half suppresses a grin when I tell him about our hassock-slumped night on the stone floor, cold as only a medieval church can be. He says it will be better this time, as there's a carpet and the heating is on a timer. He pauses. It kicks in at six, in time for morning prayers. I promise I'll be up in time.

The next day, after an almost-comfortable night, I join in with the liturgy according to the Book of Common Prayer. The murmured Reformation language, the white-plastered incense-soaked walls, and the dust motes in the glass-stained sunshine all remind me of a brief period in my twenties when I had a go at being an Anglican. I spend some time memory-mesmerised by the pull of stand, sit, kneel, repeat. Afterwards, the vicar, and his wife and children, invite me to breakfast. I sing for my sausages and explain about Father Wilfred and why I'm walking to Bardsey. It is an elenchus, the kind of question and answer where I discover more about my motivations and hopes. I leave, well into the morning, comforted that the vicar and his wife also wrestle with the question I carry. At the door she gives me two filled rolls in a paper bag and says, maybe try and enjoy yourself a bit more.

I walk for eight miles. At lunchtime I fill my notebook with words like 'sharp', and 'hard', and 'rugged'. But, despite the challenge, I think of it as a good time, although it may not be what the vicar's wife had in mind. In the afternoon I stop again and note down what I had for lunch – a packet of tomato soup and the two cheese and chutney rolls. I excavate pleasure in small things. I walk along a wooded valley carved out by a trickle of river, overwhelmed by the thrill of birdsong. A particular kind of stile stirs a memory and I check my map. At first, all seems well, but an hour later I turn off the track onto a narrow road with grass down the middle and walk into a village that is depressingly familiar. The vicar is just coming out of the lych gate.

This time they put me up on the sofa-bed in the glowing gas-fire warmth of their living room. The sofa creaks. I spend the night dreaming of collapsing Meccano sets.

Like Father Wilfred, I take children seriously, and they seem delighted to have me back. The nine-year-old looks at my map and explains where I've gone wrong. She's done a badge at Brownies and is pleased to show off her knowledge. As she tracks her finger over the bifurcation in the song-saturated woodland path, I try not to think about the loss of an entire day's walk.

I speed up, sure I can manage the change of pace despite the twinges in my knee, and over the next few days the weather helps, clearing from the merino clouds of scattered showers into the faded blue of river-washed bits of broken china. The people I encounter are still the right side of friendly, and if I can manage the burning throb of the recalcitrant knee, all will be well.

That evening I follow the coffin path to the church at Llangelynnin. My plan is to curl up in the lee of a drystone wall. I swallow two paracetamol to take the edge off the pain, simply so I can grab some sleep. It is a wretched night. In the morning, I am torn. I need a rest day – my knee is screaming – but I am increasingly behind. I hobble a miserable four miles to the Neolithic stone circles above Penmaenmawr.

That night I sleep under ink-washed skies, salt-sprinkled with stars, the moonlight shredded by clouds. I drift off to the distant bleating of sheep and wake to a realisation that it is already Holy Week. For the first time I think I might not make it by Easter. I sit for a break at mid-morning and ease off my too-new shoes. I rub the knee I'm favouring as I check the hot spots on both feet. I use up all my plasters.

A couple, walking the route in the other direction, stop to chat and eat an early lunch. Greg and Sunny have foot trouble too. Greg slips off a shoe and peels off his sock. His foot is more plaster than skin. I tell them my knees are a bit rubbish too. Eventually the older of the two men makes a face and says, if you're having a rotten time, you don't have to actually go to Bardsey, you could just catch a train back.

Temptation, thy name is Greg.

Miserable, I hobble to the station at Bangor with five minutes to spare before the afternoon train departs. I join the short queue at the ticket machine, jostled by holiday makers intent on arrivals and departures. Four minutes. One person ahead of me. I fumble my wallet and catch sight of a card I'd planned to leave on Bardsey. I take a deep breath. Three minutes. The machine asks me where I'm going. My knee twinges. Two minutes. The girl behind me tuts. I begin entering the details. The tannoy announces the imminent departure of the train. Hurry. The girl snaps her gum. I slide out of the queue. 'Change your mind, did ya?' the girl asks. She has a necklace of safety pins and white hair, not unlike mine. I put the card back in my wallet. She snaps her gum again and shifts up. I practically hop outside, skirt the town and the cathedral and head back to the hills. I have to.

That night my blackthorn-hedged sleep is broken by a drunken group singing in Welsh in the nearby lane. They manage five confident verses before they pass beyond the limits of my uneasy hearing. The indignant alarm of a robin wakes me in the morning. I swallow two more pills, tie a scarf around my knee, and hope the makeshift brace will be enough. The walk up Bangor Mountain is steep, but every day has had a path like this, where you have to remember to lift your head to see the view. I sink into the rhythm, the noise each foot-fall makes against stone, or grass, or mud. Dull percussion, in time with my heart, and the treble of hard-earned breath above.

I hum, and even this is absorbed by the wind blowing me along the ridge. The path descends and runs through a holloway, one of those sunken lanes that have been walked deep over time. In my day job I dismantle the past, the adage that archaeology is destruction still mostly holding true. Here the erosion of stone and soil is the history, the absence telling a story as vividly as any find. I count species in the hedgerow, wondering about the age of the road, and only gradually realise my steps have an echo.

The echo speeds up. Then a loud and angry hello. I think back to the warning in the shop and, like many women walking alone, I ignore the shouting and limp faster. The echo does too. For the first time on this trip, I feel apprehensive. There's another shout.

I grasp my walking poles more firmly and glance back. A man is racing along the track towards me. Red faced. Sweating. Exasperated. Waving a book. Five metres away the man bends over, planting his hands on his thighs. He breathes hard and holds the book out. It is a dog-eared leather-bound volume of

Celtic saints. 'Saint Martin gave away his cloak to a beggar,' he says. 'I hope you've got some tea'.

Mark and I sit at the side of the lane and I pull my small stove out of my bag. We discover we must have just missed each other in Bangor and he's been trying to catch me ever since. Today he has been rushing along in my wake for eight hours. He can spare another day and then he must catch a bus back. I ask him where he slept last night; he holds up his small rucksack and laughs. We stay up late that night, both of us in bivi bags propped against tree trunks, drinking tea. Mark offers to share his hip flask, but it's not my thing. He hopes I have ear plugs for when he sleeps it off. I rub my knee, swallow some more painkillers and see him frown. Bad? he asks. I hold up the almost empty packet. By torchlight he fumbles through a small first-aid kit in a plastic tub, the kind of container you get your takeaway in. He hands over three packs of fancy blister plasters and then a tube bandage. It is such a relief. I tell him he is my hero. He says he knows.

The next day we walk as we did twenty-five years ago, tidal silence and discussion, ebbing and flowing with the demands of the path. There is more slate, more grit, more signs of social instability, empty houses with blank-faced windows, tumbled-down walls, and unsecured corrugated iron roofs flailing in the wind. Mark leaves, reluctantly, in the early afternoon. He gives me an envelope and tells me to open it later, tells me to keep the book of saints too, and return it next time we meet. I remind him that if we leave it for another twenty-five years we'll be over seventy.

It is almost as if the wind knows I am running out of time,

whipping me along a stretch of beach known as the Whistling Sands. There are stories of lost mariners, pilgrims, fishermen, saints. Twenty-five years ago, we saw someone baptised in the sea not far from here. A late convert, seduced by the love and security offered by a house church. There has been no one like him on this walk, but now the devotion on his sea-washed face comes back to me, as well as the chill of the overcast day when his pastor had held him for a breath-taking length of time under the March-cold waves. To an outsider, as I rush along, I may seem equally consumed.

I arrive at the cliff top above Porth Meudwy mid-morning. On the beach below the boat is about to leave and there is a small group waiting, ready to embark. I wave as I half slide down the path in an untidy scramble. Those aboard watch my approach. As I drop my bag over the side a woman dressed for birdwatching in Gore-Tex and binoculars pats my arm and asks if I've had a good walk. I gabble something at her, only half feeling my way back into social interaction. The last time I spoke to someone was a thank you in a shop two days ago. She asks if I've come all the way on foot. When I say I have she claps her hands, the kind of enthusiasm you encounter amongst people interested in being outdoors under any conditions. An earnest man with astonished eyebrows asks about the accommodation and I tell him about my bivi bag. They give me a little round of applause.

The skipper calls our attention, and we turn towards the island. The woman sitting opposite me cries. Her mascara leaves little ink trails down her face, writing her sorrow. She's wanted to come for years. She sounds like she's apologising for whatever prevented her. Eyebrows is saying the rosary, his fingers working the wooden beads smooth. Two people set themselves apart, as far as is possible in the small launch, crammed into the narrow point of the prow. They seem over-dressed for a day on an island, no obvious gear for birdwatching or religious observations.

There are pilgrim sites that can be stumbled on in the course of a pleasant drive, like Walsingham or Canterbury. But though you might end up in Aberdaron accidentally, it is the nature of Bardsey that you have to arrive deliberately, and that you must arrive with others. At the jetty, a birdwatcher, who tells me he walked the route a few years ago, offers me a hand over the gunwale. The woman who was crying joins us, the teary ink-tracks that scribed the planes of her face now rubbed out by the salt and sun.

Both of them watch quietly as I leave a picture and Mark's envelope under a heart-shaped pebble on the altar. The envelope contains a postcard with messages from all five of my friends who made the original walk. The photograph is of Father Wilfred.

The other two are staying on the island overnight. They both shake my hand, and I am surprised how much it matters that someone is here to witness this moment. I scoop up five pebbles to send to my friends. At the jetty I drop onto a bench to wait for the boat and read some scattered notes from my diary. The pilgrimage is already slipping into the past tense. I stare over the Bardsey Sound to the beckoning mainland. More than forty years after Father Wilfred peered at me over the glint of his half-moon glasses, do I have an answer?

For now, I bend over and re-knot my laces.

BIOGRAPHIES

Faisal Ali is an Istanbul-based, Somali–British multimedia journalist who writes about East African politics, culture and religion. 'From the Desert to the Docks and Back', a reflection on his first trip to Somalia, was written between the terrace of his apartment in Istanbul and a quaint seaside café on the European shore of the Bosporus.

Julie Brominicks gave up flying years ago (she went to and from Japan by train) and writes regularly for *BBC Countryfile Magazine*, mostly about travelling in Cymru. 'The Murmuration' was written at home in the tiny caravan in Eryri she shares with her husband, to a white-water soundtrack of stream.

Sophie Buchaillard was born in Paris and lived in Bordeaux, Salamanca, Merrill (NY) and London, unintentionally settling in south Wales in 2001. Her short stories and essays have appeared in *Wales Arts Review*, *Murmurations Magazine*, *The Other Side of Hope* and *Square Wheel Press*. She co-hosts the 'Writers on Reading' podcast and tutors in creative writing. Her debut novel *This Is Not Who We Are* (Seren Books) is out in June 2022. This piece was drafted on the Eurostar between London and Paris, and finalised at her desk overlooking a sea of trees in Penarth.

Mary-Ann Constantine researches the Romantic-era culture of the Celtic-speaking countries. She lives and works in west Wales. 'King Stevan's Roads' was written in a room looking out at Mynydd Bach, Trefenter.

Siân Melangell Dafydd is an award-winning author, poet and translator who lives at the foot of the Berwyns. She was named Melangell after her great-grandmother who lived in Pennant Melangell. 'Son of a Yew Tree' was imagined where the Loing River meets the Seine, France. It was written near the Dee river, Rhosygwalia.

Giancarlo Gemin, born in Cardiff in 1962, has written two children's books, *Cow Girl* and *Sweet Pizza*, winning the Tir na n-Og awards in 2014 and 2016. His story 'Cure Time' is included in the Rhys Davies Short Story Anthology 2021. Giancarlo writes that 'The Valleys of Venice' was written 'in my study in Bexhill with my dog, Bonnie, invariably snoring on her mat beside my desk'.

Neil Gower is an acclaimed graphic artist (best known for his book jackets and literary cartography) and, latterly, a poet. Born and raised in south Wales, he now lives in Lewes and Berlin. 'From Light and Language and Tides' was hatched on three thoroughfares: Lewes High Street, Falckensteinstrasse in Kreuzberg and the M4.

Eluned Gramich is a writer and translator from west Wales. Her memoir of Hokkaido, Japan, *Woman Who Brings the Rain*, won the New Welsh Writing Awards in 2015 and was shortlisted for Wales Book of the Year 2016. Her stories and essays have appeared in *New Welsh Review*, *Planet*, *The Lonely Crowd*, *Stand Magazine* and *Wales Arts Review*. 'Carioca Cymreig' was written at the kitchen table in a house in Ely, Cardiff.

Grace Quantock is a narrative non-fiction writer and psychotherapeutic counsellor, based in Pontypool. Her writing has appeared in *The Guardian*, *The Metro* and more. She was shortlisted for The Nan Shepherd Prize and the A Writing Chance Award from Michael Sheen in 2021. 'Gone to Abergavenny' was written half on the site of the former Pen-Y-Fal Hospital and half in a council flat in Pontypool.

E. E. Rhodes is an archaeologist whose prose appears in eighty anthologies or journals, and has been recognised in fifty competitions. She won the *Intrepid Times* 'Reunions' Travel Writing Prize in 2021. 'All Among the Saints' was written between Cardiff, Worcestershire and Southwest Hertfordshire. In other words, on the M4, M40 and M25.

Kandace Siobhan Walker is a writer and filmmaker based in London. Her writing has appeared in *bath magg*, *The Good Journal* and *The Guardian*, among others. In 2021, she was the winner of *The White Review*'s Poet's Prize and an Eric Gregory Award. 'Clearances', which retraces visits to Sapelo Island, was written between Sapelo's verandas and beaches, and a green velvet sofa in South London.

PARTHIAN *Narratives*

JUST SO YOU KNOW:
Essays of Experience

Edited by Hanan Issa,
Durre Shahwar & Özgür Uyanik

'Smart, bold and fresh – these are voices we need to hear' – Darren Chetty

£9.99 • Paperback • ISBN 978-1-912681-82-2

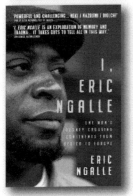

I, ERIC NGALLE:
One Man's Journey Crossing Continents from Africa to Europe

Eric Ngalle

'Powerful and challenging... neki / nazromi / diolch!' – Ifor ap Glyn

£8.99 • Paperback • ISBN 978-1-912109-10-4

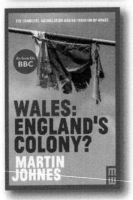

WALES: ENGLAND'S COLONY?

Martin Johnes

Wales Arts Review Book of the Year

'An engaging and thought-provoking book' – Ifan Morgan Jones, Nation.Cymru

£8.99 • Paperback • ISBN 978-1912681-41-9

PARTHIAN *Narratives*

SEVENTY YEARS OF STRUGGLE AND ACHIEVEMENT:

Life Stories of Ethnic Minority Women Living in Wales

Edited and Selected by Meena Upadhyaya, Kirsten Lavine and Chris Weedon

Foreword by Julie Morgan and Jane Hutt.
Introduction by Professor Terry Threadgold

'If you are looking for a book to inspire, then look no further.'
– Katherine Cleaver, Nation.Cymru

£20 • Hardback • ISBN 978-1913640-94-1

TAKE A BITE:

The Rhys Davies Short Story Award Anthology

Edited by Elaine Canning

Judged and with an introduction by Julia Bell

'Confident practitioners of the short story'
– Jon Gower, Nation.Cymru

£10 • Paperback • ISBN 978-1-914595-23-3

REFUGEE WALES:

Syrian Voices

Edited and selected by Angham Abdullah, Beth Thomas and Chris Weedon

Real life stories of Syrian people who have found refuge in Wales.

£20 • Hardback • ISBN 978-1-914595-30-1